A GUIDE TO
BERNARD SHAW

A GUIDE TO
BERNARD SHAW

BY

Edward Wagenknecht

AUTHOR OF "VALUES IN LITERATURE," ETC.

D. APPLETON AND COMPANY
New York   London
MCMXXIX

PRINTED IN THE UNITED STATES OF AMERICA

PREFACE

At the beginning of his excellent study of
The Views about Hamlet, my dear friend and
honored teacher, the late Professor Albert
Harris Tolman, remarked that "it behooves
one . . . who would put forth another paper
upon Hamlet to show cause at the outset why
he should not be looked upon as a public enemy."
The literature of Bernard Shaw does not as yet
rival the *Hamlet* literature, either in bulk or in
fatuity; still it is sufficiently extensive to make
a word of explanation seemly on the part of
one who seeks to offer a fresh contribution.

The primary purpose of this book is expository rather than critical. My aim has been
to gather together, within narrow and convenient compass, all the information which, in my
judgment, the student or the general reader
needs to have in mind in order to read Shaw's
plays intelligently.

The subject of my book has spoken some-
where with extreme contempt of those who

make books through re-hashing (and often garbling) what other people have already written. Yet since he, at the same time, describes himself as a crow who has followed many plows, I cannot see that he has very much ground for complaint.

My defense of the present volume is that I wrote it because it seemed to me necessary that there should be such a book. The world of Shaw has become so extensive that some such chart as this is almost indispensable. All his work is based so definitely on his theory of art and of life that to attempt to read him without some previous knowledge of his faith is to flounder helplessly in misunderstandings. Often totally mistaken conceptions of Shaw result from a fragmentary view of his work. I know this to be true from the experiences which my own students in contemporary literature courses have had. It may be objected that it is dangerous to write a book down to the level of the ordinary college student, but I do not consider myself to have done anything of the kind. After all, every one, no matter how intelligent he may be, or however great a Shavian he may ultimately become, must at one time or another read the dramatist for the first time. It is at this stage that I desire primarily to be of service. If my book serves also as a convenient summary for those who already know their Shaw, that will be all to the good.

My feeling of the vital importance of condensation made it necessary to touch very lightly on many matters of which it would have been interesting to make a fuller study. I have not had time to make an independent investigation of Shaw's literary sources. Much profitable work remains to be done in this field.

The reference list in Appendix A will, I hope, be of service in choosing plays to read. Here the prospective reader may see at a glance what is the general content of any given play or novel, and how it fits into the canon of Shaw's work.

Although, as I have said, my purpose is expository rather than critical, I have not hesitated to reveal my own opinions wherever it seemed to me that a frank expression either of dissent or of approbation might be clarifying. This is not at all because I believe it to be a matter of any importance whatever to anybody except myself whether I agree with Shaw or not. Simply, I cannot feel that insincerity or cowardice are helpful features in any piece of writing, expository or critical as the case may be.

I regret that the excellent *Dictionary to the Plays and Novels of Bernard Shaw*, by C. Lewis Broad and Violet M. Broad (The Macmillan Company, 1929) did not appear early enough for me to make it the basis of my own investigation. I have, however, in the very moment of going to press, taken a few dates from this book, which I had not been able to find elsewhere.

I desire also to express cordial thanks to my friend and colleague, Professor Glenn Hughes, for very valuable assistance in arranging for the appearance of this book.

E. W.

The University of Washington

CONTENTS

Rapprochement

BERNARD SHAW is, fundamentally, not dramatist but journalist-prophet. Quite steadily and consistently, his working life has been dedicated to the propagation of his gospel—that gospel which he believes contains power to effect the salvation of modern society and put an end to all its ills—and he has used the medium of the drama precisely as he has, from time to time, used the essay, his voice, and, in his earlier years, the novel, as a vehicle for the expression of his ideas. There are those who say that his gospel is not really his, that it is simply a patchwork of ideas, culled industriously from other thinkers, many of whom expressed the conceptions in question very much better than he does. There are others who consider it vicious, certain to effect, could it ever be put into operation, the ruination rather than the salvation of mankind. We are not concerned at the moment with either of these criticisms. The point is that notwithstanding from where he may have derived his notions in the first place, Shaw has made them his own, and he has lived by them. Very earnestly, he has set himself the task of trying to persuade his contemporaries to accept the Gospel According to Shaw, that is, in his view, to give over having their conduct regulated by prejudices and appetites, and to give God a chance to work out through them the meanings of Life.[1]

It will be seen, therefore, that the approach to Shaw must differ notably from the approach to most dramatists. Perhaps the most convenient method of distinguishing, generally, between literature and nonliterature is to say that the nonliterary product is written to achieve a definite purpose, written with an end in mind—to give information about mining in Peru, to sum up the

[1] For an especially vivid expression of this plea, *cf.* the discussion on navigation between Hector and Captain Shotover, in *Heartbreak House*, Act III, pp. 117-118.

principles underlying the study of shorthand, or to persuade us, for hygienic reasons, to give up the eating of pork, as the case may be. But just what was the "purpose" that Dickens had in mind when he wrote *David Copperfield?* Or Browning when he re-created for us the mental state of Fra Lippo Lippi? Or Eugene O'Neill when he took us with him into the weird, tortured world of *Strange Interlude?* None surely, save the very wide and general literary "purpose" of communicating a sense of human experience.

It is not the business of art to teach or to preach—it is the business of art to understand and to portray. This is the position of the orthodox literary criticism of our day, and in general it may be said that the practice of the poets, of the "makers," in every age tends to sustain it. A distinguished teacher has said that he finds it necessary, once every so often, to remind his classes that Shakespeare did not write *Othello* to teach the "lesson" that if you lie to your husband, he will strangle you in bed. Pure literature, mere literature, exists, to be

3

sure, only in theory, and there is a didactic element in many of the great achievements of the human imagination in art. But certainly this is not the literary element in the work in question, nor is it the life-giving element. *Bleak House,* surely, is not read to-day because it is an attack on the court of chancery. We Americans, at least, know little about chancery and care less. It lives because it is an interesting story of believable people existing in a vitalized world. Nor do we read *Paradise Lost* because Milton set out to

> assert Eternal Providence,
> And justify the ways of God to men.

From the modern point of view, at least, he succeeded in doing nothing of the kind, and the God of *Paradise Lost* is a miserable failure. No, *Paradise Lost* endures rather in spite of its theology than because of it, and it is the very glorification of Satan, the element which militated against the success of Milton's plan as he first conceived it, that, more than anything else, keeps the poem alive to-day. When Henry James was asked what he thought about the value of a "purpose" in a novel, he replied that the best and the least dangerous purpose, so far as he could see, was the purpose to make a perfect work of art.

Against all this, Bernard Shaw has revolted: hence the necessity for a shift of viewpoint to which I referred in the beginning. Generally one's fundamental interest in a dramatist is an æsthetic interest. The question is not, What does this man believe? Strictly speaking, the poet, as Keats perceived, has no opinions. That is why Shakespeare, who commits himself on nothing, is the perfect artist. The question is rather, What is the quality of the life experience which this man through this book communicates to me? This is true not only with romantic playwrights but even with Ibsen, even with a dramatist so wrapped up in social problems as John Galsworthy. Galsworthy is often misrepresented as having written plays with the deliberate aim to reform. He has, however, done nothing of the kind. We have his own word for it that he has not even attempted anything of the kind.[2] He writes from the literary point of view, conceiving and creating characters who live in the modern world, and who therefore must be presented against the background of that world, sharing its life and involved in its problems. But with Shaw it is the background and not the characters that are important, the moral and not the story in which he is interested. The only fair approach to his work then is through the study of the ideas which alone, in his view, give his plays their excuse for being.

It is amazing that a man whose theory of art is so patently wrong should have achieved such a place as Shaw has won. We may make all the allowance we wish for the shortcomings of his plays—their wordiness, their excessively argumentative quality, their lack of strong, absorbing story, their sometimes desperately

[2] Absolutely indispensable to the student of Galsworthy is his own discussion of his plays, printed only in the limited Manaton Edition. *Cf.* Preface to Volume XVIII (New York, Charles Scribner's Sons, 1923).

topical character, their almost entire innocence of strong, objective characterization—yet the fact remains that they are absorbing plays, and that they are being performed all over the world. Indeed, though he lacks the objective reality of Galsworthy, though he has no creative power at all in the sense in which Barrie has creative power, yet in some respects the bulk of his plays must be admitted to constitute the greatest achievement in the history of the English drama since Shakespeare's time.

May it not be well to look somewhat more closely into this phenomenon? At one time or another, Shaw has touched every important movement of his time. The student who is seeking an introduction to modern life and thought could hardly be given a more interesting assignment than the task of thinking Shaw through.

II

Biographical

GEORGE BERNARD SHAW was born in Dublin, July 26, 1856. He was the son of an Irish Protestant gentleman, a wholesale dealer in corn, whose Protestantism and whose gentlemanliness seem to have made up pretty nearly the whole of his qualifications for a battle with the world. His education was desultory. His environment he himself considered to be that of the seventeenth century. The only fortunate influence was that of his mother. She was a singer, and it was she who first opened up to her son the whole realm of music, always one of the abiding passions of his life.[3]

At the age of twenty, Shaw went to London.

[3] The best approach to an understanding of the conditions under which Shaw's youth was spent and many of his attitudes determined is through his famous article, "In the Days of My Youth," reprinted in *The Living Age*, Vol. CCCXXXII (1924), pp. 323*ff.*

At first there was no thought of a literary career. He had already made his first appearance in print, characteristically enough, in a letter to *Public Opinion,* in which he declared himself an atheist as a result of having heard Moody and Sankey in Dublin! At the outset, he essayed a mercantile career, first as a clerk in a land office in Dublin, later in London, in the employ of the Edison Telephone Company. But the work was not congenial, and thanks to the generosity of his mother, by this time established as a teacher of music in London, he was able to put it all definitely behind him in 1879.

When he did begin to write, it was natural enough, in that day, that he should turn, first of all, to prose fiction. Between 1879 and 1883 he wrote five novels. The first, significantly titled *Immaturity,* has never been published. The other four [4] finally saw the light of day, first in various socialist papers, then as books. Technically, there is practically nothing to be said for Shaw's novels. It cannot be denied, however,

[4] See Appendix A.

9

that there are many interesting pages in them, and it is particularly interesting now to see, through them, how early many of Shaw's most characteristic doctrines were developed.[5]

But for such novels England was not ready in the eighties, and Bernard Shaw has never coveted for himself the rôle of the unrecognized voice crying in the wilderness. His career as a novelist ended accordingly with the publication of *An Unsocial Socialist* in 1884. Now he was to spend nine years as a critic of parts before finally he found his place in the new drama which was so largely his own creation. In 1885, through the influence of William Archer, he was appointed a reviewer on the *Pall Mall Gazette*. In 1886 and 1887, he served as art critic on the *World*. From 1888 to 1890, he did music reviews for the *Star*. From 1895 to 1898, he

[5] *Cf.*, for example, the long speech of Cashel Byron when he is excluded from Lydia's house on the ground that a prize fighter is not fit for decent people to associate with, and defends himself on the ground that people who do far worse things than he does are let in and honored. (*Cashel Byron's Profession*, pp. 190-192.) Antivivisection, antimilitarism, opposition to hunting, football, steeplechasing, and competitive sport in general—all are present in that speech.

was dramatic critic on *The Saturday Review.* I shall speak later of the influence of this period of critical writing on his later creative work.

Meanwhile his ardent interest in social and economic problems had awakened. He was first stirred along this line when he heard Henry George speak in 1882. From Henry George, he went on to Karl Marx and *Das Kapital.* In 1884, he joined the Fabian Society, and thus fostered and developed his interest in socialism. Here he learned to argue, to debate, to think on his feet. Here also he became at once an ardent propagandist. Up to 1898, he lectured every Sunday, sometimes two or three times on a Sunday, and often several times during the week as well. In that year he suffered a physical breakdown, and since then he has been compelled to limit the number of his appearances on the lecture platform. I think it worth mentioning also that although Shaw as a playwright has watched the shekels with extreme care, his lectures have all been given entirely without monetary compensation.

Shaw has had some experience in practical administrative affairs also, not only as head of the Fabian Society in 1906 and 1907, but as vestryman and borough councilor (1897-1903), for St. Pancras district, London. He was defeated as candidate for the London City Council in 1904 because he favored improvement of the church schools, and thus alienated his free-thinking constituency.

Shaw's dramatic career began in 1892. At this time the theaters of the English-speaking world, so far as new plays were concerned, were largely given over to sentimental melodrama. While there were many great actors, and while the classics were not infrequently performed, the ability to create very fine plays in terms of the life and thought currents of the present hour seemed largely to have disappeared. The Independent Theater, dedicated to the production of just such plays, had been two years established in London, but as yet no native drama of first-rate importance was on its list. Shaw was somewhat concerned over this situation. He believed

12

Britain capable of producing serious modern plays, and finding nobody else performing the task to his satisfaction, he finally set to work to do it himself. The result was *Widowers' Houses*, a bitter attack on slum landlordism. The play stirred up a sensational discussion; ultimately it was printed and read as well as seen. As a result Shaw found himself talked about, praised, reviled. He was famous! He had caught the public ear, and from then on he never lost it.

I have now traced Shaw's biography up to the beginning of his career as a dramatist. In 1898, he married Miss Charlotte Frances Payne Townshend. The same year, his first collection of dramas, the two volumes of *Plays Pleasant and Unpleasant*, was published. Since then, his history, so far as we are concerned, has been written mainly in his work. In 1926, he was awarded the Nobel prize for literature.

The problem of sources is in his case somewhat complicated, and not all the source influences were literary in their nature. The movements with which he has been connected are so many and have been spread over so many countries that in several cases the precise indebtedness of one thinker to another cannot be determined. The perfect artist, the perfect technician, in Shaw's view, is the composer Mozart, and he considers Mozart to have had a larger influence on the structure of his work than any English dramatist with the exception of Shakespeare. His devotion to Wagner finds expression in his book, *The Perfect Wagnerite,* an interesting, even if not always very convincing, exposition of *The Ring of the Nibelungs* in terms of a revolt against nineteenth century industrialism. From Michael Angelo he learned to include persons of genius among his dramatis personæ. Not for nothing, you see, did he spend several years as a critic of art and of music. In the Preface to *Man and Superman,* he lists Bunyan, Blake, Hogarth, and Turner as the four Englishmen above all others between whom and himself he discerns a spiritual sympathy. Others mentioned in this Preface are Goethe, Shelley, Schopenhauer, Ibsen, William

Morris, Tolstoy, and Nietzsche. Although he does not mention them here, Dickens, Molière, and Samuel Butler must not be omitted in any list of the influences upon Bernard Shaw.

III

Dramatic Theory

As we have seen already, Shaw did not turn, naturally and inevitably, to the dramatic form. With him the play is never an end in itself; it is only a means to an end. This special point of view must always be kept in mind in judging his plays. Primarily, they are not plays: they are tracts in dramatic form. In spite of his own great sensitiveness to beauty, I think it is not too much to say that Shaw fears art and distrusts it except as it is controlled by some strong ethical purpose. 'Way back in *Cashel Byron's Profession,* Lydia's father warned her to be careful of all artists except very great artists. And when Sir Patrick, in *The Doctor's Dilemma,* denounces the tendency of his age to seek an escape from life through art instead of finding satisfaction in life itself, there can be

16

no doubt that the character is speaking for Shaw.

In short, Shaw regards social criticism—especially the criticism of current morality—as the outstanding function of all art. In other words, the artist is, before all else, a prophet. He sees new movements, revolts, and ideas before others are able to give coherent explanations of them, and through concentrating them in a work of art, he clarifies their meaning. It is precisely the conception which Tennyson set forth in the lines called "The Poet." Shaw frequently speaks of his plays as immoral. He glories in their immorality. One completely misunderstands him here if one fails to realize that he is giving a special meaning to the word "immoral." He does not mean that his plays are unrighteous. Rather he is using the word in its etymological sense; that is "immoral" which is contrary to established *mores* or customs. In this sense, the Eighteenth Amendment—probably the most righteous piece of legislation ever passed by a great nation—might be accurately designated as "immoral." In the face of the modern dictum that art should never be didactic, Shaw replies uncompromisingly that it should always be didactic. Indeed he goes further than this: he carries the war into the enemy's country. It is not enough that art should be didactic; it should also be religious. And, in his view, great art always is.

His preoccupation with criticism and with purpose has sometimes led Shaw to ridiculous extremes in his æsthetic judgments. Consider, for example, his statement that journalism is the highest form of literature, or his famous notion that photography is a greater art than painting because in photography the idea counts for all and mere technique is nothing. These statements represent the logical outcome of the Shavian viewpoint; one only wonders how a man with so keen a sense of humor could permit himself thus to be tricked into making the *reductio ad absurdum*. One of the worst passages in all literary criticism is surely that, in the Preface to *The Irrational Knot*, where Shaw

ranks Byron and Oscar Wilde in the first order of literary merit and Shakespeare, Scott,
Dickens, and Dumas in the second, on the ground
that while Byron and Wilde made no constructive
contribution to morality, they at least offered a
criticism—they did not take their morality
ready-made!

All these ideas are developed specifically in
connection with Shaw's criticism of the theater;
they find practical application in his own plays.
And here again we see the influence of his long
apprenticeship as a critic. Most playwrights
develop their theories to meet the exigencies of
a particular situation. Shaw approached his
task in something of a doctrinaire spirit: his
ideas were all formulated in advance. From
the very beginning he rejected the dominant
notion that the function of the theater was entertainment. To him the theater meant what it had
meant to the Greeks, what the Church means to
the devout Englishman. He thought of himself
as standing in a line of apostolic succession.
His task was to enlarge the souls of his hearers

by centering their attention on something outside their own petty interests.

Especially did he revolt against romantic melodrama; particularly did he dislike the theme of sexual love. Take Edmond Rostand, the great apostle of romance in the modern theater, place him alongside of Bernard Shaw, and you have the poetry and the prose of the drama placed in the sharpest juxtaposition possible.

In the famous Preface to *Three Plays for Puritans,* Shaw explained his opposition to the sex obsession on the stage. Sex cannot be treated realistically in the theater, he declared. Even the naughty play never has the courage of its vices. The assumption that sex is the only subject of general interest which can be made to appeal to a miscellaneous audience is fallacious; witness the example of the preachers and the politicians who have so definitely succeeded in interesting people in abstract ideas. To those who reply that this cannot be done on the stage, he cites the example of Molière and of Shake-

speare, both of whom succeeded in writing great
plays in which sex has, generally, a very
subordinate rôle.

So much for purpose. What now of technique? Technically, Shaw does not claim any
considerable originality. His methods are
largely the methods of Molière; he admits that
he has "lifted" more than one character from
the pages of Dickens. There is no doubt surely
that the *impression* is often that of something
new. The beginning of *Saint Joan*, for example
—Baudricourt's angry cry of "No eggs?"—
seems startlingly original, but it is Shaw's im-
pudence which creates the impression; technically, there is nothing here that is in any way
unusual. He has always been quick to seize the
novelties of the age and put them into his
plays, with the result that unintelligent observers
have frequently attributed to him an originality
which belongs instead to his period. When
Man and Superman was produced, the use of
an automobile on the stage was the subject of
widespread comment, and *Misalliance* comes

just as close to bringing on an airplane as the limitations of the theater will permit.

These are, of course, details. There are larger matters. In *The Quintessence of Ibsenism*, Shaw attributes technical originality to Ibsen on the ground that for the exposition, situation, and unraveling of the older drama, he substituted exposition, situation, and *discussion*. Certainly he himself has greatly encouraged this tendency of contemporary drama, frequently at the expense of his special *bête noire*, the plot. In an interview he once pretended to believe that the use of the old dramatic term, "argument," meant the same thing for the standard playwrights that it means in our speech to-day. They were not writing stories; they were writing arguments! His own plays are so full of discussion that the ideas continually overflow the forms that were designed to contain them. Consequently we must have a preface. Often the preface is as long as the play; sometimes it is three or four times longer. And *Pygmalion* has even a prose fiction sequel tacked on to it, in which we learn whom Eliza finally married and what were the conditions of her life after the final curtain dropped.

Now, strictly speaking, a dramatist has no right to do this. If he cannot express his ideas within the medium that he has chosen, it must mean either that he has not mastered its possibilities or that the effects he seeks to secure by its means are not legitimate. The only other explanation would be that he is intoxicated by the sound of his own voice, in which case it might be well for him to learn the wholesome virtue of self-restraint. Ibsen and, in our own day, Eugene O'Neill, both of whom have so consistently refused to expound their plays, may leave us in greater doubt than Shaw does of their exact meaning but it cannot be denied that they show greater respect for the integrity of their art.

Shaw's excuse, of course, is that the idea and not the form is what interests him. He intends his plays to be read as well as seen; he cannot believe that any well-written play will yield its full meaning from theatrical representation alone. Consequently, he has developed stage directions to a remarkable extent, intending through them to give the reader something like the same interpretation that the spectator would get from ideally gifted performers. Sometimes the stage direction becomes an essay; for example, the long discussion of paupers and vagabonds, prisons and capital punishment, at the beginning of the third act of *Man and Superman*. Sometimes it is a fully developed character sketch, like that of Mrs. George in *Getting Married*.

With regard to the form of his plays, Shaw has no settled practice. His ideal seems to be in each case to allow the material itself to determine the divisions in question. There are plays like *Cæsar and Cleopatra* in the traditional five acts, while, on the other hand, *Getting Married* is presented without any break whatever. In the Preface to *Getting Married*, Shaw professed conversion to what he called the Greek form in drama, declaring that this form of unity was more or less inevitable for the highest type of serious plays. This conversion, if genuine, was not permanent. *Saint Joan* is not divided into acts at all: instead there are six "scenes" and an epilogue.

In spite of his consistently serious purpose—he is perhaps the most consciously ethical of all modern writers—Shaw has worked through comedy and not through tragedy. *The Doctor's Dilemma*, alone among his plays, he calls by this solemn name. This is partly because of his ebullient temperament, necessarily finding fuller scope in comedy, but it is much more because of his optimism. As one of his best interpreters, Miss Renée M. Deacon, has suggested: "Comedy, considered in its essence, represents the forces of life as opposed to the forces of death, the latter, in a greater or less degree, forming the subject of tragedy." Shaw himself dissents from the usual opinion that tragedy is a higher dramatic form than comedy. It is only because man the warrior has been more interested in death than in life that this error ever got itself turned loose in the world. He loathes the general shambles effect which is usually attained in the last act of an Elizabethan tragedy, and he raises his voice in another unpopular cause when he defends the much-abused happy ending.

Indeed, if it were not for Shaw's tremendous optimism, he might have been less a propagandist and more an artist than he is to-day. Like H. G. Wells, he has tremendous faith in the perfectibility of the human species. Both these influential writers, though they agree that practically everything is wrong now, see nothing fundamentally unadjustable in the nature of human society. If we will only give over a few of our insane and irrational habits and consent to accept the suggestions offered by Mr. Wells or by Mr. Shaw, as the case may be, all our problems will be solved! Wells changes his panacea pretty often. In one book he will be discovering the Unknown God, in another it will be an educational reform that is called for, while a year or two later, it may be only a knowledge of history and an historic sense that can save us. Shaw's teachings have been more consistent, more carefully formulated in advance, but his spirit is at least equally hopeful. In this respect, both Wells and Shaw differ notably from their great contemporary, the pessimist John Galsworthy. Galsworthy's social sense is quite as keen as theirs, his sympathy is, if anything, deeper, but for him the source of maladjustment lies not in any temporary political and economic arrangements but deep in human nature itself, and, much as he would like to do so, he cannot persuade himself that there is any lasting cure.[6] Consequently he is satisfied to present: he offers no panacea. It may very well be that it is Galsworthy's pessimism alone that has saved him from propaganda and given him to art.

Shaw's critics urge that he is continually preaching, that all his characters are himself and are used merely as mouthpieces for his own ideas. These charges are, in the main, just. Shaw himself admits that they are just, but he is not for a moment disturbed by them. Frankly

[6] *Cf.* Preface to *A Commentary and Other Essays*, Manaton Edition, Vol. XVII.

he recognizes his inability to escape from himself, to avoid building his puppets in terms of his own temperament and experience. He has created one great character—G. B. S.—and in play after play he performs infinite variations upon it.

IV

Shaw and Shakespeare

IT is in connection with Shaw's dramatic theory
that we must consider his attitude towards Shakespeare, for the one is determined by the other.
Ever since the appearance of that flamboyant,
journalistic heading, "Better than Shakespeare?" in the Preface to *Three Plays for Puritans* in 1901, much nonsense has been talked
and written about the matter of Shaw's attitude
towards Shakespeare. First of all, it should be
made clear, I think, that Shaw knows his Shakespeare and that he appreciates him. Has he not
said that he believes Shakespeare to have been
a man very much like himself?—which, by the
way, is exactly what Shakespeare was not. And
how, from his own point of view, could he pay
a higher compliment? For the Elizabethans in
general he has indeed but little respect. There
is too much of

> sound and fury,
> Signifying nothing

about them. He would cry, as does the Queen
to Polonius:

> More matter, with less art.

But Shakespeare was better than the rest of the
Elizabethans, capable indeed of much better
work than any that his contemporaries allowed
him to do. Occasionally, to be sure, he tried
to write plays involving social problems, such
plays as *All's Well That Ends Well, Measure
for Measure,* and *Troilus and Cressida.* This is
the phase of Shakespeare's work that Shaw
values most. But the seventeenth century was
not ready for these plays; therefore Shakespeare
was forced, in spite of himself, to dish up romantic nonsense like *As You Like It* and lewd
witticisms like *Much Ado About Nothing.*[7]

But Shaw's quarrel with Shakespeare goes

[7] It is good evidence for Shaw's abiding interest in Shakespeare that he has always fought valiantly for the performance
of Shakespeare's plays in their entirety and as he designed
them. In this connection, see his amusing letter to John
Barrymore concerning the latter's production of *Hamlet,* in
Barrymore's *Confessions of an Actor* (Indianapolis, The Bobbs-
Merrill Company, 1926).

deeper than this. What he really does feel and lament in him is the lack of any constructive and synthetic philosophy of life.[8] In other words, he cannot forgive Shakespeare for being an artist, instead of a philosopher, a moralist, and a reformer. Shakespeare, he charges, gives us analysis instead of synthesis, diversity instead of unity, entertainment instead of interpretation. He tests life consistently by the vulgar hedonist test, and when life cannot be justified in this way, he becomes a pessimist. His spirit is secular, not religious.

As Shakespearean criticism, all this is absurd. It simply betrays Shaw's desperate contemporaneousness, his lack of historic sense, his inability to distinguish between the age of Elizabeth and his own. Brilliancy of perception cannot atone for lack of information where questions

[8] For a somewhat similar reaction, see *The Letters of William James* (Boston, Little, Brown and Company, 1920), II, p. 336. "Was there ever an author of such emotional importance whose reaction against false conventions of life was such an absolute zero as his?" Quoted in Albert H. Tolman, *Falstaff and Other Shakespearean Topics* (New York, The Macmillan Company, 1925), p. 42, where there is a good general discussion of the problem involved.

of scholarship are involved, nor was this statement ever better illustrated than by the Preface
to *The Dark Lady of the Sonnets,* an admirably
vigorous and infinitely diverting account of the
problem of the Sonnets but one which betrays
at every point a fundamental ignorance of the
real questions involved. Shaw swallowed Frank
Harris' ridiculous maunderings over Shakespeare, and therewith inevitably proceeded to
build a mansion on the sands. As for the impudent, conceited figure which is labeled Shakespeare in the play itself, that is simply a rather
amusing caricature of Bernard Shaw.

Yet I do not believe that further study in the
field of Shakespearean scholarship would fundamentally modify Shaw's temperamental reaction to the great Elizabethan. He has simply
called attention once more to the sharp, clean-
cut distinction between two points of view with
regard to art—to the difference between those
who see it as a direct vehicle for the interpretation of life, and those others who are well satisfied if by its means they may simply recall and

illuminate the varied beauties of the human scene. Shaw is evidently on this side of the fence, with Dante and Milton to keep him company; Shakespeare, Keats, with a host of others, are in the opposite pasture. My own position on this matter has perhaps already been made clear. At this point it may suffice to say that since great works have been produced under both inspirations, I think it conceivable that the world may possibly be able to hold the adherents of both theories for a little while longer.

In moments of levity, Shaw often misspeaks himself. Seriously I do not believe he has ever considered that he is a greater playwright than Shakespeare. What he does claim is that because he is living three centuries later, he necessarily has something to say which Shakespeare, in the nature of the case, could not have said. The mere fact that, in spite of his consciousness of the many disagreements between Shakespeare and himself, he should have been so much drawn to him, interested to devote so much attention to him, is good testimony both to Shake-

33

speare's power and to Shaw's own sensitiveness
to literary values. There can be no question
that, fallacious though it is, Shaw's Shakespeare
criticism has actually persuaded many people to
read Shakespeare critically and with an open
mind, to apply the same tests, the same standards to his work that they apply to the work of
others. Shakespeare, like the Bible, has everything to gain and nothing to lose from such a
change. Although Shaw is here perhaps symp-
tom rather than cause, there is no doubt that
there has been of recent years a vast improvement in the spirit of our Shakespearean criticism.
Personally I see no signs that the faculty of
appreciation is being destroyed.

V

The Historical Plays

THERE is a special point to be made with regard to Shaw's dramatic theory in connection with the historical plays. As in his characterizations he makes no attempt to escape from the limitations of his own temperament, so here he definitely imposes upon the past the psychology of the present. In this respect, at least, Shaw and Shakespeare are in entire agreement, for the latter wrote of all times and of all countries from the standpoint of an Elizabethan Englishman.

Consequently Shaw's historical plays are, on the surface, full of anachronisms. In *Cæsar and Cleopatra,* the courtiers cry "Egypt for the Egyptians!" while the motto of Apollodorus is "Art for Art's sake." You may, if you choose, regard this as an example of Bernard Shaw's enjoying himself, and of course it is that. Only, he has always had a strange way of enjoying himself enormously and saying something very serious at the same time. What he is saying here is that human nature does not change. We have known before this of the existence of boy kings who ruled their kingdoms through advisors, but it is none the less startling when Shaw causes the young Ptolemy to break down suddenly in the midst of his grandiloquent declaration of the royal will, simply because he has forgotten what it was that he was told to say. Even more unconventional is Charles VII's description, in *Saint Joan*, of the emotions he experienced during his coronation. Perhaps Shaw is not the first man to realize that on that famous occasion the robes may have been cruelly heavy and the consecrated oil rancid, but he is the first who has dared to put such things into a serious play.

Shaw has now given us four rather elaborate historical portraits—Cæsar, Cleopatra, Napoleon,[9] and Joan of Arc—and what we may perhaps term vignettes of, among others, Catherine

[9] *The Man of Destiny.*

36

the Great, Queen Elizabeth, Shakespeare,[10] Bishop Cauchon,[11] and General Burgoyne.[12] Two of these—Cæsar and Joan—he makes definite mouthpieces of his own ideas. Two—Cauchon and General Burgoyne—he attempts to resuscitate after misunderstanding and obloquy. But in every case, whatever Shaw's attitude, the interpretation is individual, revolutionary. Romance is forgotten. The conventional interpretation, built up through years of tradition, is ruthlessly brushed away, while the dramatist proceeds to draw the picture from his own, seemingly contemporaneous, impression of the character.

For example, Napoleon, in *The Man of Destiny*, is not a great general; he is a young corporal, twenty-seven years old. He does not understand warfare, though he is an adept in the art of swindling and shirking. He knows physical geography, can calculate times and distances, has a great power to work, and a clever under-

[10] *The Dark Lady of the Sonnets.*
[11] *Saint Joan.*
[12] *The Devil's Disciple.*

standing of human nature. He is not yet a disciplinarian, and he leads his forces into Italy only through the promise of abundant loot. He is careful of wine but careless of life, susceptible to women but brutal in his behavior towards them, a slave to ambition, hypocritically persuading himself that he is interested only in the welfare of his country. Again, Catherine, in *Great Catherine*, is German, a good deal of a savage, trying desperately to control her temper because she admires Voltaire and considers herself a philosopher. Her amorousness is not at all alluring, and not nearly so much shocking as it is common, disgusting, and funny. In drawing the portrait of Cleopatra, Shaw has remembered that at the time of Cæsar's visit to Egypt, Cleopatra was not the full-blown, worldly-wise charmer: she was a girl of sixteen. He makes her completely unscrupulous, but inexperienced, certainly no wanton, ignorant and superstitious, tyrannized over by her servants, until Cæsar arrives and teaches her some idea of how a queen ought to behave.

The most important of Shaw's historical portraits are, of course, Julius Cæsar and Joan of Arc. In the Notes to *Cæsar and Cleopatra,* many years ago, Shaw classified Joan with Lord Nelson and Charles XII of Sweden—insane all of them, captivating posterity as they captivated their own times with the peculiar quality of their insanity. One wonders just how he would reconcile that with his later conception of Joan as a great genius whose only crime was that she could see farther ahead than her contemporaries, and who was put to death by them, not at all because they were wicked but simply because they were stupid. Cæsar, alone among military conquerors, has always been one of Shaw's heroes. He stands as a type of magnanimity, a man as far above resentment as he was above sentimentality. Self-mortification Shaw objects to on the ground that it assumes that man is naturally bad and becomes good only when he denies his true nature and suppresses it. Cæsar, being naturally good, can afford to act with complete selfishness—that is, he can afford to be himself. But in the ordinary sense, Shaw does not idealize Cæsar, any more than he idealizes, say Queen Elizabeth, for example; that is, the conqueror is not represented as in any way superior to the foibles and failings of humanity. His great cross in life is the consciousness that he is growing old, and he wears a laurel crown on his head for the sole purpose of concealing his increasing baldness.

VI

The Point of View

IN speaking of Shaw's dramatic theory and practice, I have already incidentally set forth his views on many subjects. In this section, I propose next rather more definitely to examine the temperamental basis from which his work proceeds.

In *Back to Methuselah*, the Serpent says to Eve: "You see things; and you say, 'Why?' But I dream things that never were; and I say 'Why not?'" The prime significance of this passage is not that it points out the difference between the Serpent and Eve, but rather that it defines the clear distinction between Bernard Shaw and most of his contemporaries. Like the Serpent, he has always been dreaming things that never were; like her, he asks "Why not?"

Nothing could be further from the point than

the common careless assumption of unfriendly critics that Bernard Shaw is a superb thinking machine and nothing more. As I shall show in detail when I come to speak of his religion, his prime significance inheres in the fact that he is a man of faith—not a rationalist but a mystic. Temperamentally, to be sure, he is a skeptic: he cannot accept truth on authority; he must reason it out for himself. But it is this very fact that makes the outcome significant: like all sincerely religious men, Shaw believes in God because he cannot live without him. Consequently, as here in the utterance of the Serpent, he is a great visionary, but a visionary whose hope is based not on his gullibility but on his scientific-philosophical understanding of life.

For all his poetic feeling, Shaw has become the archenemy of "romance"; for all his high moral earnestness, he hates "idealism." I refer to his poetic feeling deliberately. The man who created the figure of Peter Keegan in *John Bull's Other Island*, the poet who conjured up the glamorous vision of Cæsar and Cleopatra at

the foot of the Sphinx in the desert night, the
writer who conceived the daring fantasy of the
Epilogue to *Saint Joan*—he surely cannot be supposed to lack the white splendid glow of the
imagination. We have found already that in
order correctly to apprehend what Shaw means
when he denounces "morality," we need to define the term in his own way. May it not be
that a special definition is required here also?
Let us go back to the cheap romantic melodrama
with which fiction and the drama alike were
saturated at the time Shaw began his career,
and against which he had so earnestly to fight.
This is what Shaw generally means when he
speaks of "romance" and of "idealism"—the
glorification, through false emotionalism, of
ideas and actions fallacious or reprehensible in
themselves. Such glorification he hates as he
hates drink, and for the same reason—because
it destroys reality and substitutes a dream. Like
Oscar Wilde, he believes that life imitates literature as much as literature imitates life. If we
misrepresent ourselves in art, the time will soon

come when we begin to act on the misrepresentation.

In spite of Shaw's consistently serious purpose, there prevails, even to-day, in many quarters, the wholly fatuous impression that he is a jester. For this he is indeed partly himself to blame. His self-advertisement has been and is even to-day sensational; sometimes it has approached the outrageous. Even this, however, has had a purpose. I have already said that he never at any time wished to be a voice crying in the wilderness. He enjoys the limelight; in his own way and from his own angle, he glorifies success quite as heartily as the American "go-getter" does. Moreover, altruistic motives impelled his self-advertisement. He believed sincerely that his gospel was capable of solving some of the most vexatious of human problems. It was his duty to his contemporaries, as well as to himself, to preach that gospel as widely as possible. He realized that merit in itself is recognized only by a handful: the Aimée Semple McPhersons will always draw larger audiences

44

than the George A. Gordons. He knew also that a man is permitted to speak the truth in jest long before he can proclaim it seriously. He invited everybody to his show; he provided entertainment for all. In his heart he hoped that a few would understand.

Shaw is a puritan by temperament but he is not an ascetic. In order to be an ascetic, you must first be a pessimist, as Hamlet is a pessimist in the nunnery scene with Ophelia. That is, you must have turned away from life with such repugnance and such disgust that the creative process itself is revolting to you. From Shaw's point of view, this is blasphemy. No writer has more consistently glorified sex as a clean creative power. It is precisely because of his reverence for it as the producer of life that he turns in horror from such perversions of its beauty as produce not life but death.

Thus puritanism does not mean for Shaw precisely what it meant in the seventeenth century; certainly it does not mean what it meant for the Victorians. For to-day the scientific spirit is loose in the world, and a puritanism that is merely negative, stifling, will not meet our needs. Shaw's puritanism has never caused him to shrink from life. Quite consistently he castigates the modern sin of shame. For example, he has long preached that one of the most obvious remedies for lust would be to make the naked human body such a familiar sight that it should cease to exert an aphrodisiac appeal. In *The Quintessence of Ibsenism*, he complained, half-humorously, that we do not know what any of the great characters of history really looked like. All we have is pictures of their clothes. To find out what people are really like, it is necessary to photograph them naked, as Shaw himself was photographed by Alvin Langdon Coburn. The Anglo-Saxon mind is reticent in dealing with the physical facts of life. Shaw thinks that the trouble he had with the censorship over his play, *Mrs. Warren's Profession*, showed very clearly just how much moral significance can be attached to that reticence.

One thing, however, is clear. When Shaw

pleads for nakedness, for the right to sexual experience, it is not because he cares for these things in and for themselves. Himself, he has probably had as little sensuous ecstasy as any man of his age alive. Simply, he recognizes that man has a body; he believes that the claims of the body to its own life must be honored before the spirit can soar untrammeled. Long before Freud, he perceived the danger of suppression. One may disagree with him on this point as vigorously as one cares to, but at least one should do him the justice to appreciate his point of view. In art, he has always maintained that not sensuous enjoyment but intellectual activity and moral idealism are the things to be sought.

Those who have forgotten that the Puritans, like the early Christians before them, were the great rebels of their day—out-and-out enemies of everything staid, conventional, and respectable—find it hard to reconcile Shaw's puritanism with his consuming hatred of convention. But there is no real contradiction here. As I have already pointed out, for Shaw "morality" and "righteousness" are not synonymous terms; indeed, they are antithetical terms. Morality means obedience to formulated standards imposed from without. Morality is useful only for inferior persons who are not capable of independent judgment. Therefore one must get rid of morality as a necessary prerequisite for doing, in any positive sense, what is right. This is so important that it is worth any sacrifice we need to make to achieve it, even if, like Margaret in *Fanny's First Play*, we find it necessary to go to jail in order to break down the barriers of conventional respectability.

Quite as definitely as Browning in "The Statue and the Bust," does Shaw reject the popular notion that morality consists in stifling unholy impulses. If you *want* to do evil, he would say, then by all means do it: be true to yourself. You will be less, not more, of a man if you refrain from fear of the consequences or in obedience to some ideal *external to yourself*. If, when you are set free, you turn out so badly that it is impossible for your contemporaries to

48

live with you, they will, of course, be obliged
to put you out of the way. But at least you will
have been true to yourself.

It must not be forgotten that here, as in his
speculative thinking generally, Shaw is presup-
posing a background quite different from that
against which at present we actually live. Although I do not know that he has specifically
qualified this particular doctrine, it may most
reasonably be regarded as an ideal towards
which we should strive, rather than as a cut-
and-dried rule which we can literally and im-
mediately proceed to put into operation. Shaw's
social consciousness is too keen always to allow
him to believe that any of his doctrines—which
are designed for a perfect society—could at once
be applied in our present damned society.
Always he has insisted that the fate of the individual is bound up with that of the group in
which he lives, that there can be no such thing
as a perfectly clean man in a rotten world. In
the world that we shall have to live in after the
Shavian program of social readjustment has been

put into operation, there will of course be no sexual repression and no financial want. Under these altered conditions, the Shavian precept to obey your impulses would naturally meet with fewer difficulties than at present.

What the doctrine might lead to now, in the case of completely unscrupulous degenerates, has been best demonstrated in the famous case of Leopold and Loeb. Such persons Shaw would send to the lethal chamber (although he has elsewhere argued against capital punishment). But he does not believe there are many of them. And whatever may be the verdict with regard to this doctrine, it would be unfair to leave it without pointing out that it implies tremendous faith in humanity. Unlike the Calvinist, who believes that man's impulses are naturally evil and must therefore be controlled, Shaw believes that man's impulses are naturally good and should therefore be liberated. Here, of course, he is fundamentally Christian. Set a man free to do what he likes, says Shaw, and sooner or later, he will wish to do what is good. Twice in his dramas he has exhibited for us this process of liberation. In *The Devil's Disciple*, there was no reason why Dick Dudgeon should give his life for another man, any more than there was any reason why Christ should die for the sins of the world. But when it came to a show-down, Dick found that he was powerless to take his own neck out of the noose and put another man's into it. Again, in *The Shewing-up of Blanco Posnet*, that wretched outcast did not plan to sacrifice the horse he had stolen and thereby bring himself in danger of hanging, simply to save a child's life. But when the time came, he did it, because deep down in his nature, the thing Blanco Posnet most wanted was for that child to live.

In the case of Shaw, as also in that of Browning, I find it necessary to make a distinction here between the consequences of absolute self-expression *to the individual* and the consequences *to society*. From the purely ethical standpoint, few will deny that the man who refrains from evil because he lacks the courage of his vices

51

is even lower in the moral scale than he who does evil. The point is that ethics cannot ever be considered for its own sake—as if good and evil existed in a vacuum. Like æsthetics, ethics needs to be considered in close connection with the practical problems of human life. And there is no denying that repression, whatever it may do to the individual, may sometimes be a very comfortable thing for those who have to live with the creature who is repressing himself! Personally, I feel that Shaw's precept is, in this case, based on a rather more absolute faith in human nature than the evidence tends to warrant. It is a piece of romanticizing as flagrant as some of those against which he has revolted.

What Shaw's teaching on the question of repression really amounts to in its practical application now would be virtually this: If your heart is inclined to evil, then purge your heart, or else admit that whatever conduct may be induced by external considerations, you are an evil man. On this basis, it is easy to see why all religions have genuine conversions to their credit, while ethics alone is so curiously powerless to alter human conduct. The ethical teacher holds up an ideal *external* to the sinner and bids him to do thus and so. The religionist goes to the heart of the problem always, insisting that the sinner himself must be made over. "A new heart also will I give you, and a new spirit will I put within you: and I will take away the stony heart out of your flesh, and I will give you an heart of flesh." [13]

Bernard Shaw is not usually considered a great lover of his kind. He is not satisfied with humanity as it is: he is continually trying to make it over. And in the process he often finds it necessary to castigate us, none the less painfully because wholesomely. Yet he has given his life to scheming for the good of the world, and it is quite possible that we might estimate him more accurately on this score if we were able to separate benevolent passion from mere mawkish sentimentality. Shaw himself has made that separation; indeed, he does not be

[13] Ezekiel 36:26.

53

lieve that the two are compatible. He has perceived that the man who weeps often satisfies himself with weeping; he does not find it necessary to stretch out his hand in help. Himself he does not weep: he gives. He sheds no tears over human ills. On the contrary, he sets his brain to work to find some way to relieve them.

One might suppose that Shaw's vegetarianism, his hatred of vivisection, his opposition to prize fighting, hunting, and all other forms of sport which inflict cruelty and which involve violence, would alone be enough to establish his sympathetic nature. With English critics, especially, all this is likely to work the other way. It is "abnormal," just as Shaw's refusal to drink alcohol and to smoke tobacco is abnormal. All through Mr. G. K. Chesterton's writings on Shaw there runs the note of stupefied wonder, the half-pitying, half-non-comprehending fear that something must be seriously wrong with a man who refuses to make a sewer of himself with a smoke-stack on top of it. "Bernard Shaw is a vegetarian," remarks Mr. Chesterton, "more because he dislikes dead beasts than because he likes live ones." Well, Mr. Chesterton seems to have forgotten Androcles, as well as Peter Keegan in *John Bull's Other Island*. Peter is quite in the Saint Francis of Assisi tradition, not only in his attitude towards animals, but in his sense of the unity of life, and he is a great visionary in his glorious dream of a heavenly city.

Beyond Shaw's pity for humanity is something finer—a reverence for humanity and a sense of brotherhood. His very sharpness is a compliment to you: he takes it for granted that you can stand on your own feet, that you can bear the truth, that you do not ask to be coddled. We ourselves are, in his view, the highest expression thus far of God. Humanity is continually striving to become divine.

VII

Some Aspects of the Shavian Social Gospel

I N the preceding section, we have considered
in a general way the spirit of Shaw's teaching.
It is now time to examine somewhat more con-
cretely certain definite aspects of his specific
plans for the reconstruction of society.

All these are intimately bound up with his
socialism—a very individual thing, differing in
many ways from the socialism of Marx. I cannot, of course, undertake to expound it in an
article like this, which is perforce confined to
Shaw's creative writing.[14] A few of the ideas
which play a large part in his dramas must, however, be referred to.

Of these, the first is Shaw's frank and unconventional attitude towards money. In his gospel,

[14] Shaw's studies in socialism are listed in Appendix B.
The latest and most comprehensive is *The Intelligent Woman's
Guide to Socialism and Capitalism* (1928).

it is not the love of money which is the root of all evil: it is the lack of money which is the root of all evil. Indeed, the love of money, with all the problems it brings with it, is itself determined and conditioned by the difficulty which most people have in getting their fair share of it in our capitalistic society. Without money, decency is impossible. In *Pygmalion*, Doolittle is quite ready to sell his daughter for fifty pounds, and when he is rebuked for his lack of morality, he replies that morals are too expensive for him to bother with. Similarly, Ellie, in *Heartbreak House,* is ready to sell herself to Boss Mangan when she learns that she cannot have Hector.

It must follow then that so long as the capitalistic system remains, our first duty is not to be poor. This we owe not only to our own souls but also to our fellow men, for as soon as we become poor, we are a charge on the community. Under a sanely organized socialistic society, every man's income would, of course, be guaranteed, and the income of the nation would thus be divided in equal shares. Indeed, the socialistic state will realize what we do not realize: that if the right to life is sacred, then the right to an income must also be sacred, for life cannot be supported without means.

This of course does not mean that under socialism men will not have to work. Indeed, this is just what it does not mean. Under socialism, every one will have to work; our present huge parasite classes will be done away with. Consumption without equivalent production is theft. Simply, under socialism, a man's work will have no connection with his income. Leisure, like wealth, will be distributed on a basis of equality.

Besides poverty, the special objects of Bernard Shaw's attack have been punishment, militarism, and marriage laws. It is along these lines that he proposes immediate remedies.

Shaw's ideas on punishment are set forth in the Preface to *Major Barbara*, and again in the pamphlet, *Imprisonment*. Theoretically he is forced to recognize the right of society to protect herself, even if she finds it necessary to take life in order to achieve it. But for our present system of punishment, whether by death or by incarceration, he has no use whatever, for here the ideal seems to him to be punitive. Murder is bad. Execution is, if anything, worse, for it involves the will of the whole community—not merely the will of a single criminal—in the infliction of death.

Imprisonment makes criminals: it can never cure them. Shaw cannot persuade himself that, with all the cruelties that have been committed in the name of the law, the world is any better to-day than it would have been if there had been never a prison or a gallows in it. In *The Devil's Disciple*, Dick Dudgeon tries to explain to Judith Anderson just how her love for her husband helps him to be a good man, while her hate for Dick Dudgeon helps him to be a bad one. It is senseless to punish men for being abnormal. We should cure them if possible: if not, they must be destroyed.[15]

[15] One of the most stirring passages in modern drama is that in which Cæsar explains to Cleopatra the futility of punishment and vengeance. Once begin to avenge an injury and you are weaving an endless chain of crime. The only way really to avenge an injury is to forget it. *Cf. Cæsar and Cleopatra*, Act IV, p. 100.

1894.

As far back as *Arms and the Man*, Shaw began his attack on war, proceeding here on the assumption that in order to discredit war, one must first ridicule it and strip the glamour off of it. He always knew that there are higher duties than patriotism. The mere fact that you were born in a country does not in itself make it the finest country on earth. That wise man, O'Flaherty, V.C., blames patriotism for war, and declares that patriotism must be destroyed before lasting peace can come. In *Major Barbara*, Barbara practices nonresistance with courage and humor, and it works. Bill Walker is driven almost mad by it. He does not relent towards Rummy, nor is he sorry for what he has done to her—for she pays him back hatred for hatred. But Jenny Hill's forgiveness outrages him, inflames his conscience, and compels him to seek readjustment and reconciliation.

In his personal attitude towards his own country—or rather, his two countries, Ireland and England—Shaw has acted out his patriotic ideals. It is hardly necessary to point out the satire of England and English institutions which runs all through his works. He castigates the English for their moral cowardice, their hypocrisy, their intellectual laziness, and their filthy habits.[16] In the Preface to *John Bull's Other Island*, he rises from satirist to prophet in his bitter denunciation of the massacre at Denshwai, Egypt, in 1906.

Towards Ireland, Shaw has been hardly less critical. He believes in home rule, to be sure, but not so much because he regards it as valuable in itself as because he considers its achievement a necessary prerequisite to the accomplishment of more important things. As it is, the energy which should go into vital matters of life and art is all absorbed in agitation. Perhaps when Ireland is really free, she will forget about her freedom.

With the military system without which our present system of international relationships cannot be maintained, Shaw has no patience what-

---

[16] See especially the long passage put into the mouth of Napoleon in *The Man of Destiny*, Act II, in *Plays Pleasant and Unpleasant*, pp. 212-213.

ever.[17]   It is wasteful; it is wicked; it creates a special class of parasites and incompetents. The heroism involved in war does not hoodwink him into overlooking the essential brutality of war itself.[18]

During the World War, Bernard Shaw cannot be said to have rendered any great service to the cause of peace, though, to be sure, he did not, on the other hand, go out of his way to support the cause of war. Contrary to the usual opinion, his famous pamphlet, *Common Sense about the War*, was not a pacifist document. It was Shavian; it was impudent; but essentially it surrendered the pacifist cause. The most that can be claimed for it is that it made the fire eaters thoroughly angry. Shaw to-day is not especially proud of his war record, nor do I,

[17] See "Down with the Soldier," in the Preface to *John Bull's Other Island*.

[18] Perhaps Shaw's best pronouncement on the question of militarism is his splendid burlesque of the agitation for military preparedness in the amusing topical sketch, *Press Cuttings*. It would be impossible that the arguments of the militarists could be more effectively ridiculed, their hollowness and asinine stupidity more mercilessly shown up. See especially the dialogue between Mrs. Farrell and General Mitchener (*Translations and Tomfooleries*, pp. 168-169).

for one, see any reason why he should be. He himself has pointed out on numerous occasions that had he lived in an earlier period, he would probably have been martyred. Well, he might have had his chance some time between 1914 and 1918, but I cannot see that he rushed forward with alacrity to embrace his fate. Certainly he manifested no such inspiring courage as we, here in America, had the privilege of seeing in Miss Jane Addams or in Dr. Edward A. Steiner. Here, as always, Shaw was the thinker, aloof, self-possessed, a little removed from the vulgar theater of conflict. Perhaps, like Erasmus in another day, he felt he was not worthy of martyrdom.

There remains the problem of marriage. Shaw's treatment of sex as a religious force—the theme of *Man and Superman*—belongs to the next section. The practical applications of his view must, however, be presented here.

In Shaw's view, life invented sex for the purpose of carrying on the race. It is to this aspect of life that sex should be confined. The cleavage between man and woman does not run all through art and life for him as it does for some of us, extending—as in the case of Dante—clear to the throne of God. For Shaw the higher reaches of life are sexless. There is nothing in Shaw's plays that better reveals his attitude on this point than the wonder of Liza in *Pygmalion*, when she learns that Higgins is not going to make love to her. He has taken her into his house and cared for her: what else could she expect? Higgins tries painfully to explain that to him she is a human being, not a female organism, and that her claim upon him consists in that. In other words, Shaw seeks to substitute reverence for humanity in general for the passionate absorption in one person which is the essence of love. He hates the jealousies, the subterfuges, the pettinesses of love. They consume the energy that belongs to God. In Shaw's plays the lovers always admit to each other that they have loved before, and that their happiness does not depend upon their possession of the beloved.

For Shaw, the worst of all the lies that have

been told in the name of love are those that
glorify the home. All through his plays, the presentation of the relations between parents and
children is unsympathetic, and it is always evi-
dent that Shaw is on the side of the children. He
regards every child as a fresh experiment on the
part of the Life-Force to produce a perfect man.
So far as possible, the experiment should be un-
controlled; he vitiates it who attempts to impose preconceived ideas upon it. If you object
that children must be trained, he replies that
nobody has as yet discovered how to train them.
All the methods so far devised lead to the horror
of present-day conditions; all result in the fail-
ures that we all of us are. It is only fair to
give the Life-Force a chance to produce something better if it can.[19]

At present, marriage laws seem to Shaw to
embody every conceivable fallacy in the relations between the sexes. Generally, marriage
is regarded as the most righteous of our institutions, the only effective possible bulwark

[19] For this problem, see the Preface to *Misalliance*.

against the tides of licentiousness. In his view, it is in itself the quintessence of licentiousness, making possible a far larger amount of sensual indulgence than could be obtained under any other plan. Worse than this—in these days of small families—is the glaring fact that marriage is no longer fulfilling the purpose for which it was designed. Instead, it has degenerated into a mere carnival of personal pleasure. It inhibits both the adventurous and the contemplative life: a married man cannot, in decent humanity to those dependent upon him, risk his life for an ideal as an unmarried man can. A contract for better, for worse, Shaw regards as positively immoral and an encouragement to all sorts of wickedness. In order to be successful in marriage, people must be quite independent of each other financially, and marriage must be dissolvable like any other partnership.

Theoretically Shaw goes the whole way in his "liberal" attitude towards sex. All human beings have a right to sexual experience. Every woman has a right to motherhood, whether she is married or not. All this seems to me as impractical as John Milton's theories concerning divorce. If all men were like Milton, if all men were like Shaw, it may be that all this charming "liberality" would work out successfully. Even then, I confess I have my doubts. That it would not work at all in a world in which most men are—what they are, certainly none save the completely innocent can assume. Milton was an "innocent" if ever there was one loose in the world, and in this particular connection, Shaw is but little more sophisticated. Both men, in the name of morality, and from the highest possible motives, would open up the way for a reign of unbridled indulgence.

In practice, of course, Shaw's sexual morality is quite a different thing. He himself is married, though he does not believe in marriage, just as he himself is a capitalist, though he does not believe in capitalism. One man cannot remake society; he can only declare his convictions in the hope that, by and by, he may persuade his contemporaries to agree with him, and then all may make the experiment together. As conditions are to-day, Shaw has repeatedly declared, illicit unions are far more tyrannous, much harder to escape from than the legalized unions. So long as the marriage laws remain on the statute books, marriage will remain almost inevitable for all decent, self-respecting people who contemplate a union which involves property and children.

VIII

Bernard Shaw's Religion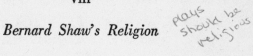

From the literary point of view, I regard *Saint Joan* as Bernard Shaw's greatest play. Not far behind it, in my estimate and in my affections, is *Androcles and the Lion*. Neither is a great historical drama, for both betray Shaw's inability to orient himself, but both have greater vitality, both bring me a stronger sense of *katharsis*, than I find anywhere else in his work. For the understanding of his ideas, however, Shaw's most important plays are *Man and Superman*, 1903, and *Back to Methuselah*, 1921. For our purpose, these two plays are one. It is here that we shall find the fullest and completest expression of Shaw's doctrine of creative evolution, the heart of his religion and of his teaching.

For Shaw, God is the Life-Force, a fierce

Will-Power behind the universe, in whose grip we all of us are. He is the God of creative evolution, and Shaw insists that he was also the God of Jesus Christ. Unlike Jesus, however, Shaw does not think of God as a personalized Power. He—or, more properly, It—is a Force, a Force seeking ever to express itself through mankind and the world. Ever since life began, this Force has been organizing and expressing itself always in higher and higher forms. At the present time, the highest expression that it has achieved is in the brain of the thinker, the philosophic man. Shaw accordingly summons humanity to cease being a passive instrument in the power of the Life-Force and itself undertake the work of direction. This is the task that humanity was brought into the world to do.

Beyond this, Shaw has not attempted to define his God. Definition imposes limitations, and this is something he has no desire to do. When the Captain in *Androcles and the Lion* asks Lavinia what God is, she replies that to know that would make us gods ourselves.

It will be seen then that, both in conception and in execution, Shaw's God differs radically from that of the orthodox Christian. Though Shaw's spirit is much closer to the spirit of Christ than that of many of those who call themselves by His name, the coldly logical method he chooses for the exposition of his ideas would commend them little to the great Galilean. For Jesus, personality was the key word of the universe, and it is in terms of personality that His religion has always been apprehended. The medieval Catholic saw God in the Virgin and the Child. The modern Protestant is conscious of the personal leadership of the man Jesus. In other words, here are concrete symbols, appealing definitely to human emotion. What nonsense to suppose that any one will relinquish the Father God to transfer his allegiance to an unconscious Life-Force!

Shaw's God is not Being: he is Becoming. Shaw rejects immortality; he breaks with the tradition of historic Christianity altogether. Yet I do not see how any one, whatever his theology, could read Bernard Shaw's religious writings without coming to feel that here is a man who, comically inadequate as his own theology may be, is yet on fire with zeal for the God whom none of us understand, yet with whom the whole significance of our lives—if they have any significance—is bound up. Forgetting questions of theology, the Roman Catholic and the Salvation Army captain alike may join hands with Bernard Shaw on the simple ground of religious zeal.[20]

The connection between *Man and Superman* and *Back to Methuselah* was noted by Shaw himself in the Preface to the later play. In *Man and Superman*, proceeding first through the study of sex, by way of the Don Juan legend, he was already trying to work out his gospel of creative evolution. Being then at the height of his career, and in full possession of his comic powers, he was, he tells us, carried away by his own enthusiasm, and developed the parable so joyfully

[20] *Cf.*, in *Androcles and the Lion*, Lavinia's masterly exposition of the fundamental unity of all religious feeling, Act I, pp. 15-16.

and to such an extent that few perceived the serious purpose at the heart of it. Now, in his age, in *Back to Methuselah,* he tries to make the point clearer and more austere. This time Don Juan is forgotten and sex is no longer a primary matter. We begin at the beginning, in the Garden of Eden.

Briefly, *Man and Superman* is simply the record of how Ann Whitefield, a "helpless" orphan, got the man whom her instinct told her she wanted as a husband for herself and a father for her children. Jack Tanner did not want to marry Ann, but all his objections were useless in the face of the woman in whom the purpose of the Life-Force was concentrated.

It must not be supposed that Shaw takes an unfavorable view of Ann. Although he declares that a woman seeking a husband is the most unscrupulous of all the beasts of prey, he does not mean that to be taken as a slur. It is for no petty purpose of personal gratification that Ann wants Tanner. Woman's business is to carry on the race. To fulfill her function, she has need of man: consequently there is nothing for it save for her to set out and get him. Her purpose is not her husband's happiness nor yet her own; both are simply serving the needs of nature. If necessary, she will sacrifice his gifts and her own life to the attainment of this purpose.

Just where the conception of the Superman came from, it is not important to inquire. The idea occurs, of course, in Nietzsche, but Shaw insists that the influence of Nietzsche on his work has been grossly exaggerated. In Wagner's Siegfried, he did find an artistic expression of the Superman, and it is in *The Perfect Wagnerite* that you will find perhaps the fullest elaboration of the idea. Obviously, Shaw cannot describe the Superman to us. The very essence of the conception is that he shall be something infinitely beyond anything that we of to-day can conceive. The process of producing him, obviously, must be through sexual selection.

Shaw's friendly critic, G. K. Chesterton,

makes two comments on the Shavian ideal of the Superman which it is interesting to consider. The first:

If Nature wishes primarily to entrap us into sexual union, then all the means of sexual attraction, even the most maudlin or theatrical, are justified at one stroke. . . . The justification of Ann, as the potential mother of Superman, is really the justification of all the humbugs and sentimentalists whom Shaw had been denouncing as a dramatic critic and as a dramatist since the beginning of his career.

This is false. Promiscuous sexual selection has not yet produced the Superman and it never can. Maudlin humbugs and sentimentalists are not in the frame of mind in which he can be begotten. He must be bred scientifically and according to law.

The other comment is no less fallacious:

In one of his least convincing phrases, Nietzsche had said that just as the ape ultimately produced the man, so should we ultimately produce something higher than the man. The immediate answer, of course, is sufficiently obvious: the ape did not worry about the man, so why should we worry about the Superman?

75

Obviously, because natural selection unaided did not do a very good job when it produced us. The Shavian ideal is to improve on the process. The ape did not worry about the man for the simple reason that in him the Life-Force had not yet sufficiently attained consciousness to make it possible for him to plan ahead. Now, since we represent a higher stage, Shaw thinks of our duty as including the direction of a process which the ape could not direct. Possibly the results may be happier under this arrangement.

So far then we come through *Man and Superman*. In *Back to Methuselah*, the stage is infinitely widened. This immense dramatic contrivance really consists of five plays, stretching from the Garden of Eden onward "As Far As Thought Can Reach," that is to A.D. 31,920.

Appearing in 1921, *Back to Methuselah* came in on the full tide of the reaction against Darwinism which followed the World War. Like the Fundamentalists in the Christian Church, Shaw holds Darwinism, with its soulless doctrine of national selection, responsible for the calamity of battle. The senseless competition, the striving one with another, the ruthless brutality, the appeal to force in the faith that the fittest will survive—when we held up these standards in the World War, we were simply imitating what we had been taught was the method of nature.[21]

To the question whether or not sufficient evidence has been accumulated to prove the truth of Darwinism, Shaw gives specifically little attention. As a matter of fact, he does not believe that Darwin proved his case. But convince his mind that Darwin did, and you do not know your Bernard Shaw if you imagine that thereupon he will become a Darwinian. Here, if anywhere, I may reënforce the statement I have already made—that he has not glorified intellect at the expense of the other elements in human life. Is this then blind dogmatism, refusal to

[21] For another effective statement of the destructive nature of the Darwinian theory, see the chapter, "Darwin: The Destroyer," in Gamaliel Bradford's *Darwin* (Boston, Houghton Mifflin Company, 1926). John Fiske stated the opposite point of view long ago in his *Through Nature to God*.

face unpleasant facts, and has Shaw here himself fallen into a pitfall whose danger all his life he has proclaimed? Not at all! Man has always believed because he must, because he cannot live without faith. "Though there be no God to hear my evening prayer," wrote Marie Bashkirtseff, "yet I pray to Him every night in despite of my reason." The deepest purpose of humanity is the will to live. This transcends, includes, supersedes everything else —including intellect; for intellect is not greater than life: it is a part of life, and the whole is greater than any of its parts. If then it can be shown that the Darwinian theory leads to race suicide via the avenue of war, then that is all the refutation that Darwinism needs. Life will not admit a philosophy that involves its own destruction.

For his own theory of creative evolution, Shaw goes back of Darwin to Lamarck. In a word, the difference between them is that for Darwin the organism is the helpless sport of forces operating upon it, while Lamarck gives the organism itself a share in the direction of its own evolution: crudely stated, creatures change because they want to. Consequently Samuel Butler's objection to Darwinian evolution, that it banished mind from the universe, does not apply here, nor need the Lamarckian believe that the normal condition of life is one of chronic warfare.

Having rejected the old legends of Christianity, Shaw feels it necessary to create some new legends for this religion of creative evolution. *Back to Methuselah* is an attempt to supply some of these legends. It is necessary to say a word or two about them.

In the first play of the Methuselah cycle, "In the Beginning," the Serpent teaches Eve to conceive children as a means of renewing life. Imagination, then, is the beginning of creation. Woman must will to tear a new life out of her own before the first child can be born. Birth was invented for the purpose of taking the burden of endless life off the individual. In the second act, after Eve has become disgusted with Cain and his ways, she admits that the process has gone too far. Her grandchildren now die before they have sense enough to know how to live. Finally she places her hope for improvement in the artists. They go on, ever learning and creating: they do not want to die.

The second play, "The Gospel of the Brothers Barnabas," presents England after the War. The theory is propounded that men can establish three hundred years as the normal human lifetime, if only they care enough for it to will it and to work towards it. This is the quite serious revolutionary proposal of *Back to Methuselah*. At present, take off the time we spend in preparation, and we have only a short time to work before our powers begin to decay. To get a race of men really capable of solving the problems that confront our civilization, it is necessary to develop a longer-lived race. Three hundred years, of course, is not the end; it is only a way station. Ultimately men will live much longer than three hundred years, but this is as ambitious a goal as Shaw thinks it well to set up now.

In the third play—A.D. 2170—"The Thing Happens." Many changes have taken place. England is now ruled by a president. The public service is manned by Chinese and educated negresses, these having shown a capacity for government which has been denied the English. The style of clothing has changed. People stop working at forty-three. It is possible to see as well as hear over the telephone. Ibsen has been proclaimed a saint. And the gift of lengthened life has actually been given to some of the characters from the second play. Longevity is still unorthodox, however, and those who have achieved it do their best to conceal the fact. The Archbishop, for example, has had to pretend to be drowned several times.

"The Tragedy of an Elderly Gentleman"— A.D. 3000—shows the process at a higher stage of development. The capital of the British Empire has now been moved to Bagdad. People are divided into primaries, secondaries, and tertiaries, according as they are living their first, second, or third hundred years. The elderly gentleman's tragedy is that he dies from the strain of contact with these people. Even Napoleon almost drops dead when the oracle is unveiled.

Finally, we reach the conclusion of the series —A.D. 31, 920—which is "As Far As Thought Can Reach." The process has now been completed. Children are born out of eggs at the stage of development at present attained in the seventeenth year. During the next four years, they go through what is now the full span of mature earthly life. Then, at the point where human beings now die, they begin to live. The Ancients—the people who really count—are hairless, naked, ugly, living a life of pure thought. Sleep has been abolished. All sensuality has been eliminated. Arts and sports alike have been outgrown. The Ancients have a direct experience of life: therefore they have no need of art. Life is no longer limited to three hundred years—you simply live on until some accident makes an end of you. The movement of life is away from all dependence upon matter. Ultimately even heads may be done away with. A vortex of thought, a whirlpool of pure intelligence—this is the goal. In no other utopia do we get so far away from the flesh.

Personally I find *Back to Methuselah* most interesting at the two extremes. "In the Beginning" is a fascinating human drama, with vitalized, understandable characters, while "As Far As Thought Can Reach," unattractive as it is, fascinates through the mere daring of its conceptions. The three other plays I find somewhat dull, certainly, in their inspiration, miles below the level of Shaw's best work. "The Gospel of the Brothers Barnabas," especially, is filled with topical allusions that are already beginning to date. But on the thought side, *Back to Methuselah* is undoubtedly Shaw's great gift to his age.

Two points in connection with Shaw's religion deserve special emphasis in closing. The first is the intensity of his faith. His God is not almighty in the sense in which the Christian God is almighty, but never for an instant does Shaw doubt that the day is His. Continually, the note recurs in his plays: God is not dependent on humanity: if you will not do His work, He will make some one or something that can. God's call to humanity, then, is an inspiration, a challenge. To be used for God's work is an opportunity, not a dismal, tiring duty. God has paid humanity the compliment of asking it to work with Him. If humanity chooses not to accept that invitation, it will be thrown on the scrap heap, and the cosmic process will move on.

The other point is Shaw's own eagerness for work, for service. This is best brought out in the picture of hell in *Man and Superman*. Hell is no place of torture; it is a country where everything is beatific, except that there is no duty there, no obligation, no task. Anybody can go to heaven who wishes to go there: the damned are in hell because they prefer it. All who love illusion rather than reality, all who seek their personal happiness before the welfare of the race—these are in hell. All who are amusing themselves instead of lending their best powers to the advancement of humanity—these are the lost souls. Time and again, Shaw has rejected for himself any personal happiness that does not carry with it the uplift of humanity. Like Swift, he longs to be worn out when he dies, to go out of the world having given to it everything that is in him. The light that is his, he has set on a candlestick that it may shine forth and give light to all who are in the house.

IX

Envoi

T HIS then is the Gospel According to Shaw. My own attitude towards it, I have by this time made sufficiently clear. As I leave Shaw now, I am not conscious of any desire to emphasize either our agreements or our disagreements. I am conscious only of a great admiration for his zeal, his humanity, his high courage—and a hope against hope that somehow these qualities may emanate from his work to society at large, more definitely than they seem yet to have done.

As for the future, a wise man has said that "Of all the forms of human error, prophecy is the most gratuitous." Yet if we may reason from analogy, and from our knowledge of those who have proceeded along similar lines, it will be difficult, I think, to persuade ourselves that most of Shaw's plays will have anything but an historic interest very far beyond his own time. They who stake their all on ideas in the world of letters die generally with the vitality of the ideas that they express. The only thing of unchanging interest in literature is that poor human nature which Shaw for one has tried so hard to change. Whether the future will consider Shaw to have been, as it were—as John Bunyan was—an artist in spite of himself, whether the parables and the figures that he created will seem in the far-off days to have vitality enough to float his ship in spite of the heavy load of impedimenta it will by then be carrying, is, of course, a question which only the future can answer.

George Bernard Shaw is not greatly interested in the answer to that question. If others pick up the torch when he is forced to drop it, and carry it onward, bringing the future a much grander light than any that his eyes were able to endure, he will be satisfied.

APPENDIX A

REFERENCE LIST OF SHAW'S WRITINGS [1]

NOVELS

CASHEL BYRON'S PROFESSION, 1882. The story of a noble prize fighter—incorruptible, chivalric, clean in body and mind—who loves a lady of culture, and who is finally accepted by her, because she feels that, on the whole, he will make a more decent husband and a better father than any "gentleman" she knows. Technically, the novel is naïve, extremely episodic in the first part, and concluding with a very precise, catalogue-like account of just what became of everybody. Coincidence too is employed freely but this with a distinctly knowing, and therefore burlesque, effect. The character drawing is good and the dialogue lifelike and convincing.

IRRATIONAL KNOT, THE, 1880. A study of marriage between classes—Edward Conolly, a worker of genius, and Marian Lind,

[1] All Shaw's works are published in America by Brentano's, New York. The dates in the following list refer to composition, not production or publication.

a society girl. The marriage fails, not at all because Marian's husband is coarse, or in any way below her, but simply because she cannot rise to his ideal of dignity and service. The wife's first assertion of individuality comes when she elopes with another lover. This experiment is a complete failure, but though her husband cherishes no animosity, he realizes when she returns that she has not been born again, not sufficiently declassed to have overcome the handicap of her early training; hence their marriage relations are not renewed. The novel is definitely experimental: neither characterization nor action is sharply enough accented, nor is the teaching made as emphatic as possible. Conolly and Elinor McQuinch both represent the Shavian critic of polite society, so conspicuous in the plays. Susan Conolly's death from excessive champagne drinking presents a typical Shavian temperance sermon.

LOVE AMONG THE ARTISTS, 1881. A long, plotless novel, based on the idea of illustrating the difference between genuine and make-believe artists. The real artists in the book are Owen Jack, a composer, and Aurélie Szczymplica, a Polish pianist. Jack, though at one time he weakens and hankers for a wife, soon regains his balance and realizes that such things are not for him. Aurélie yields to the love plaint of Adrian Herbert, a weakling quite adept at explaining his artistic aims and quite powerless to carry them out, but the very qualities that have made for her success as an artist make her impossible as a wife. Mary Sutherland, to whom Adrian had been engaged in the first part of the book, is a sane young English girl with an interest in beauty which for a time she is tricked into regarding as a touch of the creative instinct. But the gift will not be forced. The other artist of the book, Magdalene Brailsford, is of a lower and different order: through courage and perseverance, she forces her way, despite much opposition, into a popular stage success. Structurally, nothing can be said of *Love Among the Artists:* it has no structure. Some of the speeches, especially Jack's, provide vehicles for Shaw's familiar impressions of marriage, music, and art. In its treatment of love and marriage, the book is, however, distinctly uneven. The absence of sentimentality occasionally produces some very true and courageous writing, as in some of the scenes between Aurélie and Herbert. Elsewhere the characters behave like puppets with no emotional nature whatever.

UNSOCIAL SOCIALIST, AN, 1883. The unsocial socialist is Sidney Trefusis. The child of monopolists, oppressed by his wealth, he dedicates it to the task of spreading socialism, and when he finds that his love for his Jewish wife is interfering with his life work, he simply leaves her. Though Shaw gives Trefusis many of his ideas, he is careful to disclaim responsibility for the harsher features of his conduct. Trefusis's letter to the author, appended to the narrative, is a kind of burlesque Shaw preface. Though the book contains many interesting ideas, Shaw has seldom been so unreal, has seldom so unscrupulously forced his characters to serve as mere mouthpieces of his own ideas, as in the unconvincing picture of Trefusis at his wife's funeral, and again in the ridiculous wooing scene between Trefusis and Agatha Wylie.

PLAYS

ADMIRABLE BASHVILLE, THE, 1901. A dramatic burlesque version in blank verse of Shaw's novel, *Cashel Byron's Profession,* written to prevent the dramatic rights of the novel from falling into other hands. The effect of bombast and heroic attitudinizing on the *Cashel Byron* material may well be imagined, and the play is not any less funny for the occasional interjection of delightfully *malapropos* passages from Shakespeare and Marlowe. A "Note on Modern Prizefighting" is appended, in which Shaw contends that the Queensberry rules have not modified the brutal character of this sport, and connects his opposition to prize fighting with his whole philosophy of life.

ANDROCLES AND THE LION, 1912. Starting from the story of the lion in *Sandford and Merton, Androcles and the Lion* is a study of the Roman Empire's political persecution of the Christian religion. Despite all fantasy and exaggeration, the analysis of primitive Christianity and its types may be pronounced fundamentally realistic. Spinthio, the blackguard, has joined the sect after an evil career, not at all because he has experienced a change of heart, but simply because he has snatched at the popular interpretation of Paulinism—that whoever dies a martyr will escape hell, no matter what his life has been. Ferrovius, a man of fierce passions, forgets Christ when brought face to face with the gladiators and reverts to his real type. As a reward for his murderous valor, he is invited to join the Prætorian Guard. This, of course, is allegory: the surrender of Ferrovius is the surrender of the Church to the State in the person of the Emperor Constantine. But not all the Christians are unworthy. Androcles, the little tailor, is charming. Without heroics, he is a thoroughly honorable man, and his attitude towards animals is one of the humanest things in modern literature. Lavinia is a noble, thoroughly sane, high-minded woman who would be a credit to any dramatist.

ANNAJANSKA, THE BOLSHEVIK EMPRESS, 1917. A "turn" for the Coliseum Variety Theatre. Strammfest and Schneidekind, nominally in the service of the Revolution but secretly loyal to the Panjandrum (Tsar) and the old order, are astonished when the daughter of the Panjandrum turns Bolshevik and advocates war to save the country through binding all elements together in a common cause.

ARMS AND THE MAN, 1894. Under the austere inspiration of the *Æneid*, Shaw has written a farcical comedy, the profoundly serious purpose of which is to strike a blow against war by stripping all the false glamour of military heroics and patriotism away from it. This is achieved through a very realistic study of the unheroic Captain Bluntschli, Swiss volunteer in the Servian army, who carries chocolate instead of bullets and who believes that it is a soldier's duty to keep out of danger as much as possible. To be sure, the play also contains an old-fashioned, slightly Byronic military hero, Sergius, but unfortunately for the romanticists, Sergius is much less efficient than Bluntschli. Raina, the Bulgarian girl in the case, illustrates the deleterious effect of cheap romantic fiction on conduct. Really a practical, clear-sighted young woman by nature, she wears romantic spectacles to look at life, until at last Bluntschli brings about her awakening and her disillusionment. The love scenes between Sergius and Raina show us two lovers talking sentimental nonsense because they think it is expected of them, instead of saying the things they really feel.

Arms and the Man was set to music by Oscar Strauss as *The Chocolate Soldier*.

AUGUSTUS DOES HIS BIT, 1916. A topical sketch, castigating the British governing class, personified in Lord Augustus Highcastle, recruiting sergeant, for its stupidity, incompetence, and selfishness during the World War.

BACK TO METHUSELAH, 1921. Discussed in the text, section VIII.

CÆSAR AND CLEOPATRA, 1898. Instead of a love tragedy à la Shakespeare, Shaw has aimed at a realistic picture of Egyptian intrigues at the time of Cæsar's visit to Egypt. This does not mean that there is any attempt at historic verisimilitude, simply that the great passions of a celebrated "affair" are all reduced in scale until they become comprehensible, everyday emotions. The play is rich in action and *mise en scène,* unusually so for Shaw. It is also less definitely and closely organized than most of his writings; it bears less directly upon a single theme. The desert scene in which Cleopatra, asleep in the arms of the Sphinx, first meets Cæsar, is probably the most glamorous in all Shaw. For the characterization, see the text, section V.

CANDIDA, 1894. Already one of the classic comedies of the English theater, *Candida* lives by virtue of its distinguished character portrayal. There is little propaganda. The principal characters are three: the Reverend James Mavor Morell, a Christian socialist, a perfectly sincere man, desperately intoxicated with his own rhetoric; Eugene Marchbanks, a young poet, physically a desperate weakling but impertinently courageous in spirit; Candida (Mrs. Morell), a womanly woman of abundant common sense, fully aware of her husband's weaknesses and loving him for himself and not for his sermons. There are three minor characters also: Candida's father, Burgess, who has been compelled by law to pay his workmen a living wage, and who now comes to Morell to boast of his magnanimity and exhibit himself as a model employer; Prossy, Morell's stenographer, worshiping her employer from afar; and the Reverend Alexander Mill, Morell's curate, a greedy, lazy, imitative little man. The crisis of the play comes through Marchbanks, who falls in love with Candida, denounces Morell as a windbag, and proffers himself as Candida's true mate. Candida settles the question by giving herself to the weaker of the two—that is, to the mighty Morell. This conservative outcome won many plaudits for Shaw as the defender of the home, but it is only accidentally that he became that in this instance. For it is made perfectly clear that with Candida it is love—not the marriage vow which is meaningless without it—love and a man's appeal to a woman's sense of his need, upon which the home must be built. The "secret in the poet's heart" at the close of the play is probably his glad knowledge that he is big enough to live without love.

CAPTAIN BRASSBOUND'S CONVERSION, 1899. Shaw calls *Brassbound,* "A Play of Adventure." More accurately and specifically, it is a satirical melodrama. Against the picturesque background of Morocco, we have smugglers, sheiks, cadis, savages, and the United States Navy to take the situation in hand at the exactly opportune moment and settle everything in accordance with the highest principles of justice and chivalry. Nowhere more definitely than in this play and *The Devil's Disciple* is the satiric aspect of Shaw's vision of the human comedy presented, and the contrast between heroic posturings and petty reality more clearly brought out. The situations throughout are extremely conventional and melodramatic; the way in which they are twisted into ironic commentary is in some ways suggestive of Gilbert and Sullivan. The best character is Lady Cicely Waynflete (written for Ellen Terry), a most disarming combination of charming manners, combined with an uncanny faculty for absolutely dominating any group into which she comes.

DARK LADY OF THE SONNETS, THE, 1910. A plea for a National Theater, put into the mouth of Shakespeare upon an accidental midnight meeting with Queen Elizabeth on the terrace at Whitehall. The play is built upon the exploded theory that Mary Fitton was the Dark Lady.

DEVIL'S DISCIPLE, THE, 1897. In 1777, the high faith and ardor of Puritanism had passed in New England, and the claim to superior rectitude had decayed into the narrowest sort of intolerant cruelty. Out of this atmosphere comes Dick Dudgeon, chivalrous, kindly, self-sacrificing—a man whose deepest need is his hunger for God. But since he knows God only as the cruel inspiration of his flint-hearted mother, he has no alternative save to avow himself the Devil's disciple. For him, the Devil represents the outcast, the champion of kindness and love, the principle of rebellion against heartless and oppressive authority. For the religious implications of the play, see pp. 48-51.

DOCTOR'S DILEMMA, THE, 1906. "A Tragedy." Sir Colenso Ridgeon, having discovered a cure for tuberculosis, is forced to choose between two applicants, one a thoroughly unscrupulous young genius and the other a stupid, middle-aged, but thoroughly good and honest doctor. He chooses to save the doctor. Moreover, being himself in love with the scoundrel's wife, he turns him over to a bungler, whose ministrations greatly hasten his end. Although Shaw has no sympathy with Dubedat and his creed of art for art's sake, his play is an argument against entrusting such powers to physicians that one of them, by no means a monster, might easily find himself in Sir Colenso's position. The first act is an amusing satire on medical vagaries.

FANNY'S FIRST PLAY, 1910. Though he calls it a potboiler, *Fanny's First Play* is still one of Shaw's most amusing productions. The play itself, which Fanny has written, and the frame—in which Shaw discusses himself, quite in the manner of Molière, at the same time ridiculing the attitude of the English dramatic critics towards his work—are about equally amusing. The play itself is a protest against the smugness of conventional respectability.

FASCINATING FOUNDLING, THE, 1909. "A Disgrace to the Author." The Lord Chancellor makes a match between an orphan in chancery and a strong-minded young suffragette lady whose arms simply ache to gather a beloved object to her breast. Not important.

GETTING MARRIED, 1908. A full-length play in one act, designed to illustrate the barbarous condition of the British marriage laws, as well as the confusion of mind which exists in England concerning marriage. Among others, we have Edith and Cecil, who, having learned that legally one party to a marrage is responsible for the acts of the other, rebel on their wedding day; Reginald Bridgenorth, who, simply because his wife wants to divorce him, is compelled to give her grounds by abusing her and then going off with a woman of the streets; Soames, the strictly ascetic priest, who detests every sort of marital union; and Lesbia, the "old maid," who desires children, and is eminently fitted to rear them, but who resolutely refuses to burden herself with a husband for the sake of getting them. Taken without its Preface, the teaching of the play may be pronounced conservative. So many difficulties are experienced in drawing up the "contract," that the young couple finally slip off quietly and are married, regarding the orthodox form of tyranny as, on the whole, less burdensome than any other that might just then be devised.

GLIMPSE OF REALITY, THE, 1909. Intrigue in fifteenth century Italy. The motiving is none too clear, and Shaw's attempt to invest the action with metaphysical significance is not successful.

GREAT CATHERINE, 1913. A bravura piece, built around the amorous proclivities of the Russian Empress. The four very brief scenes deal with her unsuccessful attempt to fascinate a very proper English officer, a veteran of Bunker Hill.

HEARTBREAK HOUSE, 1917. Bernard Shaw's impression of Europe before the World War. He castigates its neglect of civic duty, its philandering, its romantic nonsense, its inefficient bungling capitalism, the curious combination of silly, adolescent idealism and sordid commercialism in its attitude towards marriage, its unmitigated cruelty and brutality. The details of the allegory are not always clear, but the reaction of the inhabitants of the house to the air raid at the close of the play is clearly intended to symbolize the insane, foolhardy emotionalism with which the nations met the War. Life had become such a hopeless bungle that the only interesting thing left was to flirt with death. Ironically enough, the two prudent people in the house are the very ones who are killed; the fools all come through without a scratch. When the danger has passed over, life becomes dull again, and they all hope there may be another raid to-morrow night. Most of the characters of *Heartbreak House* are either, like Captain Shotover—the mystic, stung with the horrors of life, through whom Shaw has chosen to deliver some of his profoundest oracles—definitely insane, or else, like Hector Hushabye and his wife, perilously close to the verge. Taken together with its wonderful preface, *Heartbreak House* remains a record of Bernard Shaw's war-time agony. There is an undertone of anguish not often sounded in his work.

HOW HE LIED TO HER HUSBAND, 1904.

A footnote to *Candida*, and an attempt to work out a fresh treatment of the stale triangle situation. The originality consists in the husband's rage over the implied insult to his wife when her lover—who has acted hitherto under the inspiration of Marchbanks—denies that his intercepted poems were written to Mrs. Bompas on the ground that he does not admire her "in that way." Peace is not restored until the poet confesses his passion, whereupon Bompas, taking all this as one more tribute to his wife's great charm and beauty, is happy again.

INCA OF PERUSALEM, THE, 1915. The Inca of Perusalem is the Kaiser, and the play is simply a war-time caricature, designed to ridicule Wilhelm's vanity, his bad taste, his narrowness, his contempt for others, and his bondage to convention.

INTERLUDE AT THE PLAYHOUSE, THE, 1907. A one-act play built around the embarrassment of an actor-manager at having to deliver a curtain speech. London *Daily Mail*, January 29, 1907. Not published in book form.

JOHN BULL'S OTHER ISLAND, 1904. Written for the Irish National Theatre, but rejected as not sufficiently in the tone of the Irish Renascence. The play and the Preface constitute Shaw's fullest and frankest discussion of the Irish question. The third act especially presupposes so much information concerning Anglo-Irish relations in 1904 that it is almost unintelligible to many Americans, and, I imagine, at this date not overabsorbing to anybody. What the play has—in the person of Peter Keegan, a kindly priest, unfrocked for supposed madness, with a theory that this earth is hell to which all humanity has been condemned for sins committed elsewhere, and a Saint Francis-like feeling of union with animals—is a note of mystic tenderness not too conspicuous in Shaw, a foreshadowing of *Androcles and the Lion,* or even of that splendid flowering of Shavian mysticism in *Saint Joan.* The actual plot concerns a pair of engineers who come to Ireland ostensibly to develop a Garden City—really, as Peter Keegan perceives, simply to continue the traditional English exploitation of Ireland. Doyle, though Irish by birth, is in revolt against Irish sentimental dreaming as standing in the way of progress. His partner, Broadbent, is an English muddler, completely ignorant of everything Irish, and for this very reason winning Irish allegiance—to say nothing of the only heiress in Rosscullen.

MAJOR BARBARA, 1905. Big Business and the Salvation Army. Undershaft is a maker of munitions, a mystic who glorifies death and destruction. His life is in the grip of the Life-Force; consequently, according to Shaw, he is more admirable than the namby-pamby good persons who do nothing. Major Barbara leaves the Army when she finds it accepting money from distillers and munition makers. Later she comes to see that you cannot destroy evil by running away from it. The problem of tainted money is everywhere; you can escape it only by escaping life. This theme had already been handled in *Widowers' Houses* and *Mrs. Warren's Profession.*. Shaw is saying that there is no possibility of individual salvation in a damned society. In other words, the only real salvation is social salvation.

MAN AND SUPERMAN, 1903. Discussed in the text, section VIII.

MAN OF DESTINY, THE, 1895. An attack on the romantic view of Napoleon. *Cf.* the text, section V. The scene of the play is laid in a small inn in Northern Italy, and the fable concerns a battle of wits between the "man of destiny" and a clever woman. Written for Richard Mansfield, but rejected by him.

MISALLIANCE, 1910. A long discussion in one act on such subjects as the tyranny of the family, the hopelessness of one generation trying to understand another, the impossibilities of anarchism, and the sensual horrors of sexual suppression. It is pointed only in its individual hits, and is distinctly lacking in dramatic interest. The characters are largely (in the Elizabethan sense) humors.

MRS. WARREN'S PROFESSION, 1894.

A plea for the complete economic independence of women as the only sure means of abolishing prostitution. Mrs. Warren's alternative was either to wear out her life in grinding toil or else to become a kept woman. She chose the latter alternative, and while Shaw is fully conscious of her degradation, he regards society, much more than Mrs. Warren, as the guilty party. This does not mean that the courtesan is sentimentalized, *Camille*-fashion. For Mrs. Warren is not only prostitute but procuress, and the revelation of this deeper infamy is so managed that it alienates not only her daughter but the reader as well. To-day, *Mrs. Warren's Profession*, though it is certainly Shaw's most painful production, is universally recognized as a brave plea for social house cleaning and one of the most moral plays ever written. It is difficult to realize that less than thirty years ago, Arnold Daly's attempts to present it in America were actually attended with police prosecution. In the Preface to *How He Lied to Her Husband,* Shaw strikes back mercilessly at his critics, arguing brilliantly and convincingly that they objected to his play, not because their purity was revolted, but rather because they represented the classes tied up in their interests with the profits derived, through rents and low wages, from Mrs. Warren's profession.

MUSIC CURE, THE, 1914. "A Piece of Utter Nonsense." A farcical situation beginning in nerves and ending in marriage, which is designed especially for the relaxation of two performers on the pianoforte.

O'FLAHERTY, V. C., 1915. O'Flaherty, war hero, home for recruiting, discusses the War. In the Preface, Shaw seriously pretends to have designed the play to stimulate recruiting. Without the Preface it must be taken as simply a very effective pacifist protest against war. For once the British government must be given credit for having seen through the hoax in time to reject Shaw's proffered aid.

OVERRULED, 1912. A study of marital infidelity in terms of farce comedy, which is presented as a model to future writers in the same field. One hopes the model will not be too slavishly followed, for *Overruled* is one of Shaw's least convincing productions. Even farce, to be successful, must produce that "willing suspension of disbelief" without which all forms of fiction are impossible. This *Overruled* quite fails to do. There is good fun in Mr. Juno, however, who insists that, no matter what his sins, all is well, so long as he keeps the ideal before him and does not pretend to defend his conduct.

PASSION, POISON, AND PETRIFICATION, or, THE FATAL GAZOGENE, 1905. A burlesque of Elizabethan tragedy. Unnatural and stilted speeches, fantastic names, jealous husbands administering poison, apprehensive servants, thunder and lightning, and shouts of "welcome, Death"—they are all here.

PHILANDERER, THE, 1893. Satire on Ibsenism and its detractors, with the "new woman" as a focusing point. She insists on all the privileges of man but wants to retain also all the courtesies traditionally shown to woman. She is advanced when she wants to get a man and quite conservative when she desires to give him up. The medical profession is satirized in the person of Dr. Paramore, who is convulsed with grief when he discovers that the liver disease he has recently discovered doesn't exist.

PLAYLETS OF THE WAR. See the following titles: *O'Flaherty, V.C., The Inca of Perusalem, Augustus Does His Bit, Annajanska.*

PLAYS PLEASANT AND UNPLEASANT, 1898. See the following titles: *Arms and the Man, Candida, The Man of Destiny, Mrs. Warren's Profession, The Philanderer, Widowers' Houses, You Never Can Tell.*

PRESS CUTTINGS, 1909. Splendid burlesque on the military party and the anti-suffragettes. *Cf.* the text, page 62 n.

PYGMALION, 1912. Shaw says he wrote *Pygmalion* to teach the British public the importance of phonetics. It is like him to seek thus to impose a purpose even upon a play which is comparatively innocent of one, for although Shaw's philosophy is implicit in every line of *Pygmalion*, the play is not as a whole didactic. Instead, ethical teaching is subordinated to fun making, and the interplay of character, as it should be. In this case, Pygmalion is not a sculptor; he is Henry Higgins, a philologist and phonetician. Galatea is Liza Doolittle, a dirty but respectable flower girl, and the play consists in Higgins's attempt to improve Liza's speech until it reaches the point where he shall be able to pass her off as a duchess at an ambassador's garden party. This attempt is wholly successful, but Higgins's inability to realize that the girl has a point of view of her own, and that she is something more than material for an experiment, introduces complications into the situation for which he had not bargained. Eliza as duchess is no longer fit for her old station in life, and she does not find her new one until we reach the prose fiction appendix in which Shaw tells what happened to her after the close of the play. *Pygmalion* was produced by Sir Herbert Beerbohm Tree with himself as Higgins and Mrs. Patrick Campbell as Liza. For an amusing account of its production, see Shaw's article in Max Beerbohm's memorial volume, *Herbert Beerbohm Tree* (New York, E. P. Dutton & Co. n.d.)

SAINT JOAN, 1923. One of the great achievements of the modern drama. *Saint Joan* is as brilliant as any Shaw play has ever been, but there is no trace of the "smartness" or cocksureness that disfigured so much of his earlier work. Instead it is tender, mystical, and profoundly moving, this study of genius—a touching picture of the terrible loneliness of a great soul. Much nonsense has been written about Joan of Arc, and much incense burned at her shrine, but this attempt to present her as a credible human being—not a miracle worker but a genius—is something wholly different. To be sure, the play is not medieval in its motiving. When Joan meets the objection that her voices come from her imagination with a frank admission that they do, and that that is the way in which God communicates with us, it is Shaw who is speaking, not Joan. The reasoning of the archbishop on the subject of miracles also belongs to the twentieth century and not to the fifteenth. Natural explanations are offered of such incidents as Joan's immediate recognition of the Dauphin upon her arrival at court and her leap from the tower during her imprisonment. The use of northern dialect to give the flavor of Joan's peasant origin is, to say the least, a very daring and a very questionable dramatic device. But these are minor matters. They are of no consequence whatever beside the fine exposition of Protestantism and nationalism in Scene 4 (undramatic though it is), the scrupulous honesty with which the character of Cauchon is resuscitated after centuries of Protestant obloquy, the magnificent epilogue in which Joan returns after her execution, and, above all, the splendid characterization of Joan herself. If he had written only *Saint Joan*, Shaw would still be one of our greatest dramatists. Sybil Thorndike played Saint Joan in London. In America the actresses most conspicuously identified with the part have been Winifred Lenihan, in the world première of the play, New York Theatre Guild production, and Julia Arthur.

SHEWING-UP OF BLANCO POSNET, THE, 1909. Ostensibly simply a one-act cowboy melodrama, with the scene laid in a small Western town in the United States (where Shaw has never visited), *The Shewing-up of Blanco Posnet* is perhaps Bernard Shaw's most triumphant affirmation of faith: the glad faith that God will not be defeated, that men and women, however bad they may be, are yet too good wholly to refuse to perform His Will—the Will for which He brought them into the world. Indeed Shaw virtually foreordains salvation for his sinners. Blanco did not want to sacrifice the horse he had stolen, simply to save a child's life; Feemy wanted to see her enemy hanged, not saved; the Sheriff never had any intention of rising to a crisis and standing out bravely against a blood-thirsty mob. But when the moment of testing came, they all did right and not wrong, because they were in the grip of the force which would not let them go. In England, a license was refused *The Shewing-up of Blanco Posnet*, a happy circumstance which gave Shaw the opportunity to attach to the play, by way of Preface, an eighty-four page discussion of the whole question of censorship.

THREE PLAYS FOR PURITANS, 1901. See the following titles: *Cæsar and Cleopatra, Captain Brassbound's Conversion, The Devil's Disciple.*

TRANSLATIONS AND TOMFOOLERIES,
1926. See the following titles: *The Admirable Bashville; The Fascinating Foundling; The Glimpse of Reality; The Music Cure; Passion, Poison, and Petrification; Press Cuttings.* The volume also contains *Jitta's Atonement,* a translation by Shaw from the German of Siegfried Trebitsch.

WIDOWERS' HOUSES, 1892. Shaw's first play, a merciless exposure of living conditions in the slums of London, the blame for which is placed, in characteristically Shavian fashion, not on the miserable agents to whose lot falls the dirty work of refusing necessary repairs and squeezing out rent money which is needed for bread, but upon the respectable aristocracy, which derives its income from rents, in entire blissful ignorance of the conditions which produce them. In the last act, the attack shifts to municipal jobbery. The view of human nature in this play may be called cynical. That is to say, none of the characters rise above self-interest.

YOU NEVER CAN TELL, 1897. Simply an amusing, and very long, character comedy, with characteristic Shavian types.

APPENDIX B

SUGGESTIONS FOR STUDY

RELIGION

Back to Methuselah
Man and Superman
Androcles and the Lion
Saint Joan
The Shewing-up of Blanco Posnet
Major Barbara
The Devil's Disciple

SEX AND MARRIAGE

Man and Superman
Getting Married
Candida
Misalliance
Overruled
How He Lied to Her Husband

117

WAR

Arms and the Man
Heartbreak House
Press Cuttings
Playlets of the War

POVERTY

Major Barbara
Mrs. Warren's Profession
Widowers' Houses

HISTORY

Cæsar and Cleopatra
The Man of Destiny
Saint Joan
Great Catherine
The Dark Lady of the Sonnets
The Devil's Disciple

Shaw's most important critical writings comprise the prefaces to his various plays. In addition, there are the following essays on literary and artistic subjects: *The Quintessence of Ibsenism*, 1891 and 1913; *The Sanity of Art*,

1895; *The Perfect Wagnerite*, 1898; *Dramatic Opinions and Essays*, 1906; and Preface to *Three Plays by Brieux*, 1911.

For Shaw's views on socialism and practical affairs, see: *Fabian Essays in Socialism*, 1899; *Fabianism and the Empire*, 1900; *Fabianism and the Fiscal Question*, 1900; *The Common Sense of Municipal Trading*, 1904; *Socialism and Superior Brains*, 1910; *Common Sense about the War*, 1914; How to Settle the Irish Question, 1917; *Peace Conference Hints*, 1919; Preface to Webb, *English Prisons*, 1922 (now published separately as a pamphlet with the title, *Imprisonment*); *The Intelligent Woman's Guide to Socialism and Capitalism*, 1928.

The most important book about Shaw is Archibald Henderson, *George Bernard Shaw, His Life and Works*, 1911. An interesting footnote to Henderson's biography is his *Table-Talk of G. B. S.*, 1925. Among the other books about Shaw are the following, which vary greatly in merit: Patrick Braybrooke, *The Genius of Bernard Shaw*, 1925; Richard Burton, *George Bernard Shaw, The Man and the Mask*, 1916; G. K. Chesterton, *George Bernard Shaw*, 1909; J. S. Collis, *Shaw*, 1925; Renée M. Deacon, *Bernard*

Shaw as Artist-Philosopher, 1910; H. C. Duffin, *The Quintessence of Bernard Shaw*, 1920; Augustin Hamon, *The Twentieth Century Molière*, 1915; P. P. Howe, *Bernard Shaw*, 1915; James Huneker, *Iconoclasts*, 1910; Holbrook Jackson, *George Bernard Shaw*, 1907; Joseph McCabe, *George Bernard Shaw*, 1914; H. L. Mencken, *George Bernard Shaw, His Plays*, 1905; Edward Shanks, *Bernard Shaw*, 1924; E. E. Slosson, *Six Major Prophets*, 1917. See also *Do We Agree?*, 1928 (a debate between Shaw and Chesterton, with Belloc in the chair). For magazine articles, see the *Reader's Guide*.

1. Compare Bernard Shaw as a critic of society with any or all of the following writers: Voltaire, Swift, Leopardi, Byron, Shelley, Mark Twain, Anatole France. Here are some of the factors to be taken into consideration: temperament, motives, sincerity, accuracy, methods, effectiveness. Enlarge the list.

2. Study Shaw as a writer of melodrama, especially in *The Devil's Disciple* and *Captain Brassbound's Conversion*. Are they mere melodramas?

3. Trace the stage conventions of the nine-

ties through Shaw's earlier plays. Note when he gives them a satirical twist. Does he ever follow them uncritically?

4. Are Shaw's prefaces supplementary to his plays, or are they an integral part of them? To answer this question, determine whether or not the play is completely intelligible without the preface.

5. Compare Shaw's stage directions with those of earlier dramatists. How far, if at all, does he tend to rely on stage directions for the presentation of character? Does this interfere with his presentation of character in dialogue and in action?

6. Are Shaw's characters static, or do they develop in the course of the action?

7. Make a study of three or four of Shaw's outstanding "chorus characters," *i.e.*, those who directly voice the author's point of view.

8. Are Shaw's young women "flappers"? Which of their qualities does he seem to admire? Which does he regard as the unfortunate products of unnatural constraint? (Good examples are Margaret in *Fanny's First Play*, Dolly in *You Never Can Tell*, and Savvy in *Back to Methuselah*.)

9. Compare *Jitta's Atonement* (*Translations and Tomfooleries*) with its original, *Frau Gitte's Sühne,* by Siegfried Trebitsch. What was it that attracted Shaw in the German play? What changes did he make, and what do these show about his own dramatic practice and ideals?

10. Collect Shaw's references to Dickens and formulate a statement of Shaw's attitude towards Dickens and the social service that he rendered. Then try to trace Dickensian influence through Shaw's own work. (See Shaw's suggestive analysis of the differences between Dickens and Ibsen, in *The Quintessence of Ibsenism,* page 204.)

11. Starting from Larry Doyle's description of Rosscullen (*John Bull's Other Island,* Act I), compare Shaw's treatment of Ireland with that of the Irish playwrights.

12. Granting that the value of existence lies in its quality and not in its length, what does Shaw propose to gain (*Back to Methuselah*) by lengthening the span of human life to three hundred years? How is this worked out between Parts II and III of the play?

13. Compare *Mrs. Warren's Profession* with Maupassant's story, *Yvette.*

14. Compare *Cæsar and Cleopatra* with Shakespeare's *Antony and Cleopatra* and with Dryden's *All For Love.*

15. How does Shaw's presentation of Joan of Arc differ from that of earlier writers on the same subject? Consider Voltaire, Shakespeare, Schiller, Mark Twain, Percy MacKaye, Anatole France.

16. Compare Shaw's attitude toward doctors (*The Doctor's Dilemma*) with that of Molière. (See Augustin Hamon's extensive comparison between Shaw and Molière in his *Twentieth Century Molière.*)

17. Compare Shaw's conception of the character of Cæsar with that of H. G. Wells (*The Outline of History*).

INDEX

125

INDEX

INDEX

127

INDEX

LITERARY CRITICISM AND HISTORY

SPOKESMEN: MODERN WRITERS AND AMERICAN LIFE

By T. K. WHIPPLE. Critical portraits of our outstanding American authors. Theodore Dreiser, Sherwood Anderson, Willa Cather, Henry Adams and others. "A singularly discerning collection of essays."—*Van Wyck Brooks in the New York Sun.*

THE PHILOSOPHY OF FICTION

By GRANT OVERTON. A piece of creative criticism of great originality. An outline history of fiction and a study of the comparative techniques of master novelists, including full discussions of such writers as Jane Austen, Conrad, Tolstoi, Willa Cather, and many others. "

A STUDY OF THE MODERN NOVEL: BRITISH AND AMERICAN SINCE 1900

By ANNIE RUSSELL MARBLE. A combined history and handbook of fiction of significant value written in English since 1900, offering biographical facts and critical estimates. A general survey of the novel of this period.

THE DEVELOPMENT OF DRAMATIC ART

By DONALD CLIVE STUART. An important and remarkable contribution to dramatic literature, by the Professor of Dramatic Art at Princeton University. Traces the development of the dramatist's art from its origins to its latest development in the work of O'Neill and Gordon Craig.

A STUDY OF THE MODERN DRAMA

By BARRETT H. CLARK. A Revised Edition of this book everywhere regarded as an indispensable work on the modern drama. Critical studies, bibliographies and short biographies of all important contemporary dramatists.

THE NOBEL PRIZE WINNERS IN LITERATURE

By ANNIE RUSSELL MARBLE. A study of the works and lives of the winners of the outstanding literary honor—the Nobel Prize. *Illustrated.*

D. APPLETON AND COMPANY
35 WEST 32ND STREET   NEW YORK

"The Interesting World of Words"

MODERN ENGLISH IN THE MAKING
By George H. McKnight. A richly informative account of the growth of the English language from Chaucer to the present, told with charm and sustained interest.

THE PSYCHOLOGY OF LANGUAGE
By Walter B. Pillsbury and Clarence L. Meader. A famous psychologist and an eminent linguist have collaborated to produce the first comprehensive study of the language processes.

ENGLISH WORDS AND THEIR BACKGROUND
By George H. McKnight. A very readable account of the origin, development and modern tendencies of English words.

THE WRITING AND READING OF VERSE
By C. E. Andrews. "He has written a book which can be heartily recommended to all who wish to know upon what the formal beauties of English verse are based."—*Chicago Evening Post.*

FIRST PRINCIPLES OF SPEECH TRAINING
By Elizabeth Avery, Jane O. Dorsey and Vera A. Sickels. An elementary study of the scientific principles of speech training and their practical application to the improvement of everyday speech. The book is based upon the phonetic method.

A DICTIONARY OF ENGLISH PRONUNCIATION WITH AMERICAN VARIANTS
By H. E. Palmer, J. V. Martin and F. G. Blandford. Gives in phonetic transcription a safe pronunciation of about 10,000 essential words, including permissible American and Canadian variants.

GROWTH AND STRUCTURE OF THE ENGLISH LANGUAGE
By Otto Jespersen. A history of the development of the English Language and an analysis of its salient features.

D. APPLETON AND COMPANY
35 West 32nd Street   New York